FOREWORD

The collection of "Everything Will Be Okay" travel phrasebooks published by T&P Books is designed for people traveling abroad for tourism and business. The phrasebooks contain what matters most - the essentials for basic communication. This is an indispensable set of phrases to "survive" while abroad.

This phrasebook will help you in most cases where you need to ask something, get directions, find out how much something costs, etc. It can also resolve difficult communication situations where gestures just won't help.

This book contains a lot of phrases that have been grouped according to the most relevant topics. The edition also includes a small vocabulary that contains roughly 3,000 of the most frequently used words. Another section of the phrasebook provides a gastronomical dictionary that may help you order food at a restaurant or buy groceries at the store.

Take "Everything Will Be Okay" phrasebook with you on the road and you'll have an irreplaceable traveling companion who will help you find your way out of any situation and teach you to not fear speaking with foreigners.

TABLE OF CONTENTS

T&P Books Publishing

Travel phrasebooks collection
«Everything Will Be Okay!»

T&P Books Publishing

PHRASEBOOK

— ALBANIAN —

By Andrey Taranov

THE MOST IMPORTANT PHRASES

This phrasebook contains
the most important
phrases and questions
for basic communication
Everything you need
to survive overseas

T&P BOOKS

Phrasebook + 3000-word dictionary

English-Albanian phrasebook & topical vocabulary

By Andrey Taranov

The collection of "Everything Will Be Okay" travel phrasebooks published by T&P Books is designed for people traveling abroad for tourism and business. The phrasebooks contain what matters most - the essentials for basic communication. This is an indispensable set of phrases to "survive" while abroad.

This book also includes a small topical vocabulary that contains roughly 3,000 of the most frequently used words. Another section of the phrasebook provides a gastronomical dictionary that may help you order food at a restaurant or buy groceries at the store.

T&P Books Publishing
www.tpbooks.com

ISBN: 978-1-78767-152-2

This book is also available in E-book formats.
Please visit www.tpbooks.com or the major online bookstores.

PRONUNCIATION

T&P phonetic alphabet	Albanian example	English example
[a]	flas [flas]	shorter than in ask
[e], [ɛ]	melodi [mɛlodí]	absent, pet
[ə]	kërkoj [kərkój]	driver, teacher
[i]	pikë [píkə]	shorter than in feet
[o]	motor [motór]	pod, John
[u]	fuqi [fucí]	book
[y]	myshk [myʃk]	fuel, tuna
[b]	brakë [brákə]	baby, book
[c]	oqean [ocɛán]	Irish - ceist
[d]	adoptoj [adoptój]	day, doctor
[ʣ]	lexoj [lɛdzój]	beads, kids
[ʤ]	xham [dʒam]	joke, general
[ð]	dhomë [ðómə]	weather, together
[f]	i fortë [i fórtə]	face, food
[g]	bullgari [buɫgarí]	game, gold
[h]	jaht [jáht]	home, have
[j]	hyrje [hýrjɛ]	yes, New York
[ɟ]	zgjedh [zɟɛð]	geese
[k]	korik [korík]	clock, kiss
[l]	lëviz [ləvíz]	lace, people
[ɫ]	shkallë [ʃkáɫə]	feel
[m]	medalje [mɛdáljɛ]	magic, milk
[n]	klan [klan]	name, normal
[ɲ]	spanjoll [spaɲóɫ]	canyon, new
[ŋ]	trung [truŋ]	ring
[p]	polici [politsí]	pencil, private
[r]	i erët [i érət]	rice, radio
[ɾ]	groshë [gróʃə]	Spanish - pero
[s]	spital [spitál]	city, boss
[ʃ]	shes [ʃɛs]	machine, shark
[t]	tapet [tapét]	tourist, trip
[ts]	batica [batítsa]	cats, tsetse fly
[ʧ]	kaçube [katʃúbɛ]	church, French
[v]	javor [javór]	very, river
[z]	horizont [horizónt]	zebra, please
[ʒ]	kuzhinë [kuʒínə]	forge, pleasure
[θ]	përkthej [pərkθéj]	month, tooth

LIST OF ABBREVIATIONS

English abbreviations

ab.	-	about
adj	-	adjective
adv	-	adverb
anim.	-	animate
as adj	-	attributive noun used as adjective
e.g.	-	for example
etc.	-	et cetera
fam.	-	familiar
fem.	-	feminine
form.	-	formal
inanim.	-	inanimate
masc.	-	masculine
math	-	mathematics
mil.	-	military
n	-	noun
pl	-	plural
pron.	-	pronoun
sb	-	somebody
sing.	-	singular
sth	-	something
v aux	-	auxiliary verb
vi	-	intransitive verb
vi, vt	-	intransitive, transitive verb
vt	-	transitive verb

Albanian abbreviations

f	-	feminine noun
m	-	masculine noun
pl	-	plural

T&P BOOKS

ALBANIAN
PHRASEBOOK

This section contains
important phrases that may
come in handy in various
real-life situations.
The phrasebook will help
you ask for directions, clarify
a price, buy tickets, and
order food at a restaurant

T&P Books Publishing

PHRASEBOOK
CONTENTS

T&P Books Publishing

The bare minimum

Excuse me, ...
Më falni, ...
[mə fálni, ...]

Hello.
Përshëndetje.
[pərʃəndétjɛ]

Thank you.
Faleminderit.
[falɛmindérit]

Good bye.
Mirupafshim.
[mirupáfʃim]

Yes.
Po.
[po]

No.
Jo.
[jo]

I don't know.
Nuk e di.
[nuk ɛ di]

Where? | Where to? | When?
Ku? | Për ku? | Kur?
[ku? | pər ku? | kur?]

I need ...
Më nevojitet ...
[mə nɛvojítɛt ...]

I want ...
Dua ...
[dúa ...]

Do you have ...?
Keni ...?
[kéni ...?]

Is there a ... here?
A ka ... këtu?
[a ka ... kətú?]

May I ...?
Mund të ...?
[mund tə ...?]

..., please (polite request)
..., ju lutem
[...], [ju lútɛm]

I'm looking for ...
Kërkoj ...
[kərkój ...]

the restroom
tualet
[tualét]

an ATM
bankomat
[bankomát]

a pharmacy (drugstore)
farmaci
[farmatsí]

a hospital
spital
[spitál]

the police station
komisariat policie
[komisariát politsíɛ]

the subway
metro
[mɛtró]

a taxi	**taksi** [táksi]
the train station	**stacion treni** [statsión trɛni]

My name is ...	**Më quajnë ...** [mə cúajnə ...]
What's your name?	**Si quheni?** [si cúhɛni?]
Could you please help me?	**Ju lutem, mund të ndihmoni?** [ju lútɛm], [mund tə ndihmóni?]
I've got a problem.	**Kam një problem.** [kam ɲə problém]
I don't feel well.	**Nuk ndihem mirë.** [nuk ndíhɛm mírə]
Call an ambulance!	**Thërrisni një ambulancë!** [θərísni ɲə ambulántsəl]
May I make a call?	**Mund të bëj një telefonatë?** [mund tə bəj ɲə tɛlɛfonátə?]

I'm sorry.	**Më vjen keq.** [mə vjɛn kɛc]
You're welcome.	**Ju lutem.** [ju lútɛm]

I, me	**unë, mua** [únə], [múa]
you (inform.)	**ti** [ti]
he	**ai** [ai]
she	**ajo** [ajó]
they (masc.)	**ata** [atá]
they (fem.)	**ato** [ató]
we	**ne** [nɛ]
you (pl)	**ju** [ju]
you (sg, form.)	**ju** [ju]

ENTRANCE	**HYRJE** [hýrjɛ]
EXIT	**DALJE** [dáljɛ]
OUT OF ORDER	**NUK FUNKSIONON** [nuk funksionón]
CLOSED	**MBYLLUR** [mbýɫuɾ]

OPEN	**HAPUR** [hápur]
FOR WOMEN	**PËR FEMRA** [pər fémra]
FOR MEN	**PËR MESHKUJ** [pər méʃkuj]

Questions

Where?	**Ku?** [ku?]
Where to?	**Për ku?** [pər ku?]
Where from?	**Nga ku?** [ŋa ku?]
Why?	**Pse?** [psɛ?]
For what reason?	**Për çfarë arsye?** [pər tʃfárə arsýɛ?]
When?	**Kur?** [kur?]

How long?	**Sa kohë?** [sa kóhə?]
At what time?	**Në çfarë ore?** [nə tʃfárə órɛ?]
How much?	**Sa kushton?** [sa kuʃtón?]
Do you have …?	**Keni …?** [kéni …?]
Where is …?	**Ku ndodhet …?** [ku ndóðɛt …?]

What time is it?	**Sa është ora?** [sa əʃtə óra?]
May I make a call?	**Mund të bëj një telefonatë?** [mund tə bəj ɲə tɛlɛfonátə?]
Who's there?	**Kush është?** [kuʃ əʃtə?]
Can I smoke here?	**Mund të pi duhan këtu?** [mund tə pi duhán kətú?]
May I …?	**Mund të …?** [mund tə …?]

Needs

I'd like ...	**Do të doja ...** [do tə dója ...]
I don't want ...	**Nuk dua ...** [nuk dúa ...]
I'm thirsty.	**Kam etje.** [kam étjɛ]
I want to sleep.	**Dua të fle.** [dúa tə flé]

I want ...	**Dua ...** [dúa ...]
to wash up	**të lahem** [tə láhɛm]
to brush my teeth	**të laj dhëmbët** [tə laj ðémbət]
to rest a while	**të pushoj pak** [tə puʃój pak]
to change my clothes	**të ndërrohem** [tə ndəróhɛm]

to go back to the hotel	**të kthehem në hotel** [tə kθéhɛm nə hotél]
to buy ...	**të blej ...** [tə blɛj ...]
to go to ...	**të shkoj në ...** [tə ʃkoj nə ...]
to visit ...	**të vizitoj ...** [tə vizitój ...]
to meet with ...	**të takohem me ...** [tə takóhɛm mɛ ...]
to make a call	**të bëj një telefonatë** [tə bəj ɲə tɛlɛfonátə]

I'm tired.	**Jam i /e/ lodhur.** [jam i /ɛ/ lóðuɾ]
We are tired.	**Jemi të lodhur.** [jémi tə lóðuɾ]
I'm cold.	**Kam ftohtë.** [kam ftóhtə]
I'm hot.	**Kam vapë.** [kam vápə]
I'm OK.	**Jam mirë.** [jam mírə]

I need to make a call.

Duhet të bëj një telefonatë.
[dúhɛt tə bəj ɲe tɛlɛfonátə]

I need to go to the restroom.

Duhet të shkoj në tualet.
[dúhɛt tə ʃkoj nə tualét]

I have to go.

Duhet të ik.
[dúhɛt tə ik]

I have to go now.

Duhet të ik tani.
[dúhɛt tə ik taní]

Asking for directions

Excuse me, ...

Më falni, ...
[mə fálni, ...]

Where is ...?

Ku ndodhet ...?
[ku ndóðɛt ...?]

Which way is ...?

Si shkohet në ...?
[si ʃkóhɛt nə ...?]

Could you help me, please?

Ju lutem, mund të më ndihmoni?
[ju lútɛm], [mund tə mə ndihmóni?]

I'm looking for ...

Kërkoj ...
[kərkój ...]

I'm looking for the exit.

Kërkoj daljen.
[kərkój dáljɛn]

I'm going to ...

Po shkoj në ...
[po ʃkoj nə ...]

Am I going the right way to ...?

A po shkoj siç duhet për në ...?
[a po ʃkoj sitʃ dúhɛt pər nə ...?]

Is it far?

Është larg?
[ə́ʃtə larg?]

Can I get there on foot?

Mund të shkoj me këmbë deri atje?
[mund tə ʃkoj mɛ kə́mbə déri atjé?]

Can you show me on the map?

Mund të më tregoni në hartë?
[mund tə mə trɛgóni nə hártə?]

Show me where we are right now.

Më tregoni ku ndodhemi tani.
[mə trɛgóni ku ndóðɛmi taní]

Here

Këtu
[kətú]

There

Atje
[atjé]

This way

Këtej
[kətéj]

Turn right.

Kthehuni djathtas.
[kθéhuni djáθtas]

Turn left.

Kthehuni majtas.
[kθéhuni májtas]

first (second, third) turn

kthesa e parë (e dytë, e tretë)
[kθésa ɛ párə (ɛ dýtə], [ɛ trétə)]

to the right

djathtas
[djáθtas]

to the left

majtas
[májtas]

Go straight ahead.

ecni drejt
[étsni dréjt]

Signs

WELCOME!	**MIRË SE ERDHËT!** [mírə sɛ érðət!]
ENTRANCE	**HYRJE** [hýrjɛ]
EXIT	**DALJE** [dáljɛ]

PUSH	**SHTY** [ʃty]
PULL	**TËRHIQ** [tərhíc]
OPEN	**HAPUR** [hápur]
CLOSED	**MBYLLUR** [mbýɫur]

FOR WOMEN	**PËR FEMRA** [pər fémra]
FOR MEN	**PËR MESHKUJ** [pər méʃkuj]
GENTLEMEN, GENTS	**ZOTËRINJ** [zotəríɲ]
WOMEN	**ZONJA** [zóɲa]

DISCOUNTS	**ULJE** [úljɛ]
SALE	**ULJE** [úljɛ]
FREE	**FALAS** [fálas]
NEW!	**E RE!** [ɛ ré!]
ATTENTION!	**KUJDES!** [kujdés!]

NO VACANCIES	**NUK KA VENDE TË LIRA** [nuk ka véndɛ tə líra]
RESERVED	**REZERVUAR** [rɛzɛrvúar]
ADMINISTRATION	**ADMINISTRATA** [administráta]
STAFF ONLY	**VETËM PËR PERSONELIN** [vétəm pər pɛrsonélin]

BEWARE OF THE DOG!	**KUJDES NGA QENI!** [kujdés ŋa céni!]
NO SMOKING!	**NDALOHET DUHANI!** [ndalóhɛt duháni!]
DO NOT TOUCH!	**MOS PREKNI!** [mos prékni!]
DANGEROUS	**I RREZIKSHËM** [i rɛzíkʃəm]
DANGER	**RREZIK** [rɛzík]
HIGH VOLTAGE	**VOLTAZH I LARTË** [voltáʒ i lártə]
NO SWIMMING!	**NDALOHET NOTI!** [ndalóhɛt nóti!]

OUT OF ORDER	**NUK FUNKSIONON** [nuk funksionón]
FLAMMABLE	**I DJEGSHËM** [i djégʃəm]
FORBIDDEN	**I NDALUAR** [i ndalúar]
NO TRESPASSING!	**NDALOHET KALIMI!** [ndalóhɛt kalími!]
WET PAINT	**BOJË E FRESKËT** [bójə ɛ fréskət]

CLOSED FOR RENOVATIONS	**MBYLLUR PËR RESTAURIM** [mbýłur pər rɛstaurim]
WORKS AHEAD	**PO KRYHEN PUNIME** [po krýhɛn punímɛ]
DETOUR	**DEVIJIM** [dɛvijím]

Transportation. General phrases

plane	**avion** [avión]
train	**tren** [trɛn]
bus	**autobus** [autobús]
ferry	**traget** [tragét]
taxi	**taksi** [táksi]
car	**makinë** [makínə]

schedule	**orar** [orár]
Where can I see the schedule?	**Ku mund të shikoj oraret?** [ku mund tə ʃikój orárɛt?]
workdays (weekdays)	**ditë pune** [dítə púnɛ]
weekends	**fundjava** [fundjáva]
holidays	**pushime** [puʃímɛ]

DEPARTURE	**NISJE** [nísjɛ]
ARRIVAL	**MBËRRITJE** [mbərítjɛ]
DELAYED	**VONESË** [vonésə]
CANCELLED	**ANULUAR** [anulúar]

next (train, etc.)	**tjetër** [tjétər]
first	**parë** [párə]
last	**fundit** [fúndit]

When is the next …?	**Kur është … tjetër?** [kur əʃtə … tjétər?]
When is the first …?	**Kur është … i parë?** [kur əʃtə … i párə?]

When is the last ...?

Kur është ... i fundit?
[kur éʃtə ... i fúndit?]

transfer (change of trains, etc.)

ndërrim
[ndərím]

to make a transfer

të ndërroj
[tə ndərój]

Do I need to make a transfer?

Duhet të ndërroj?
[dúhɛt tə ndərój?]

Buying tickets

Where can I buy tickets?	**Ku mund të blej bileta?** [ku mund tə bléj biléta?]
ticket	**biletë** [bilétə]
to buy a ticket	**të blej biletë** [tə blɛj bilétə]
ticket price	**çmimi i biletës** [tʃmími i bilétəs]
Where to?	**Për ku?** [pər ku?]
To what station?	**Në cilin stacion?** [nə tsílin statsión?]
I need ...	**Më nevojitet ...** [mə nɛvojítɛt ...]
one ticket	**një biletë** [ɲə bilétə]
two tickets	**dy bileta** [dy biléta]
three tickets	**tre bileta** [trɛ biléta]
one-way	**vajtje** [vájtjɛ]
round-trip	**me kthim** [mɛ kθim]
first class	**klasi i parë** [klási i párə]
second class	**klasi i dytë** [klási i dýtə]
today	**sot** [sot]
tomorrow	**nesër** [nésər]
the day after tomorrow	**pasnesër** [pasnésər]
in the morning	**në mëngjes** [nə mənɟés]
in the afternoon	**në pasdite** [nə pasdítɛ]
in the evening	**në mbrëmje** [nə mbrámjɛ]

aisle seat	**ulëse në korridor** [úləsɛ nə koridór]
window seat	**ulëse tek dritarja** [úləsɛ tɛk dritárja]
How much?	**Sa kushton?** [sa kuʃtón?]
Can I pay by credit card?	**Mund të paguaj me kartelë krediti?** [mund tə pagúaj mɛ kartélə krɛdíti?]

Bus

bus	**autobus** [autobús]
intercity bus	**autobus urban** [autobús urbán]
bus stop	**stacion autobusi** [statsión autobúsi]
Where's the nearest bus stop?	**Ku ndodhet stacioni më i afërt i autobusit?** [ku ndóðɛt statsióni mə i áfərt i autobúsit?]

number (bus ~, etc.)	**numri** [númri]
Which bus do I take to get to ...?	**Cilin autobus duhet të marr për të shkuar në ...?** [tsílin autobús dúhɛt tə mar pər tə ʃkúar nə ...?]
Does this bus go to ...?	**A shkon ky autobus në ...?** [a ʃkon ky autobús nə ...?]
How frequent are the buses?	**Sa shpesh kalojnë autobusët?** [sa ʃpɛʃ kalójnə autobúsət?]

every 15 minutes	**çdo 15 minuta** [tʃdo pɛsəmbəðjétə minúta]
every half hour	**çdo gjysmë ore** [tʃdo ɟýsmə órɛ]
every hour	**çdo një orë** [tʃdo ɲə órə]
several times a day	**disa herë në ditë** [dísa hérə nə dítə]
... times a day	**... herë në ditë** [... hérə nə dítə]

schedule	**orari** [orári]
Where can I see the schedule?	**Ku mund të shikoj oraret?** [ku mund tə ʃikój orárɛt?]
When is the next bus?	**Kur është autobusi tjetër?** [kur ə́ʃtə autobúsi tjétər?]
When is the first bus?	**Kur është autobusi i parë?** [kur ə́ʃtə autobúsi i párə?]
When is the last bus?	**Kur është autobusi i fundit?** [kur ə́ʃtə autobúsi i fúndit?]

stop	**stacion** [statsión]
next stop	**stacioni tjetër** [statsióni tjétər]
last stop (terminus)	**stacioni i fundit** [statsióni i fúndit]
Stop here, please.	**Ju lutem, ndaloni këtu.** [ju lútɛm], [ndalóni kətú]
Excuse me, this is my stop.	**Më falni, ky është stacioni im.** [mə fálni], [ky éʃtə statsióni im]

Train

train	**tren** [trɛn]
suburban train	**tren lokal** [trɛn lokál]
long-distance train	**tren** [trɛn]
train station	**stacion treni** [statsión trɛni]
Excuse me, where is the exit to the platform?	**Më falni, ku është dalja për në platformë?** [mə fálni], [ku əʃtə dálja pər nə platfórmə?]

Does this train go to …?	**A shkon ky tren në …?** [a ʃkon ky trɛn nə …?]
next train	**treni tjetër** [tréni tjétər]
When is the next train?	**Kur vjen treni tjetër?** [kur vjɛn tréni tjétər?]
Where can I see the schedule?	**Ku mund të shikoj oraret?** [ku mund tə ʃikój orárɛt?]
From which platform?	**Nga cila platformë?** [ŋa tsíla platfórmə?]
When does the train arrive in …?	**Kur arrin treni në …** [kur arín tréni nə …]

Please help me.	**Ju lutem më ndihmoni.** [ju lútɛm mə ndihmóni]
I'm looking for my seat.	**Kërkoj ulësen time.** [kərkój úləsɛn tímɛ]
We're looking for our seats.	**Po kërkojmë ulëset tona.** [po kərkójmə úləsɛt tóna]
My seat is taken.	**ulësja ime është zënë.** [úləsja ímɛ əʃtə zénə]
Our seats are taken.	**ulëset tona janë zënë.** [úləsɛt tóna jánə zénə]

I'm sorry but this is my seat.	**Më falni por kjo është ulësja ime.** [mə fálni por kjo əʃtə úləsja ímɛ]
Is this seat taken?	**A është e zënë kjo ulëse?** [a əʃtə ɛ zénə kjo úləsɛ?]
May I sit here?	**Mund të ulem këtu?** [mund tə úlɛm kətú?]

On the train. Dialogue (No ticket)

Ticket, please.

Biletën, ju lutem.
[bilétən], [ju lútɛm]

I don't have a ticket.

Nuk kam biletë.
[nuk kam bilétə]

I lost my ticket.

Humba biletën.
[húmba bilétən]

I forgot my ticket at home.

E harrova biletën në shtëpi.
[ɛ haróva bilétən nə ʃtəpí]

You can buy a ticket from me.

Mund të blini biletën tek unë.
[mund tə blíni bilétən tɛk únə]

You will also have to pay a fine.

Duhet gjithashtu të paguani gjobë.
[dúhɛt ɟiθaʃtú tə pagúani ɟóbə]

Okay.

Në rregull.
[nə réguɫ]

Where are you going?

Ku po shkoni?
[ku po ʃkóni?]

I'm going to ...

Po shkoj në ...
[po ʃkoj nə ...]

How much? I don't understand.

Sa kushton? Nuk kuptoj.
[sa kuʃtón? nuk kuptój]

Write it down, please.

Shkruajeni, ju lutem.
[ʃkrúajɛni], [ju lútɛm]

Okay. Can I pay with a credit card?

Në rregull. Mund të paguaj me kartelë krediti?
[nə réguɫ. mund tə pagúaj mɛ kartélə krɛdíti?]

Yes, you can.

Po, mundeni.
[po], [múndɛni]

Here's your receipt.

Urdhëroni faturën.
[urðəróni fatúrən]

Sorry about the fine.

Më vjen keq për gjobën.
[mə vjɛn kɛc pər ɟóbən]

That's okay. It was my fault.

S'ka gjë. ishte gabimi im.
[s'ka ɟə. íʃtɛ gabími im]

Enjoy your trip.

Rrugë të mbarë.
[rúgə tə mbárə]

Taxi

taxi
taksi
[táksi]

taxi driver
shofer taksie
[ʃofér taksíɛ]

to catch a taxi
të kap taksi
[tə kap táksi]

taxi stand
stacion për taksi
[statsión pər táksi]

Where can I get a taxi?
Ku mund të gjej një taksi?
[ku mund tə ɟɛj ɲə táksi?]

to call a taxi
thërras një taksi
[θərás ɲə táksi]

I need a taxi.
Më nevojitet taksi.
[mə nɛvojítɛt táksi]

Right now.
Tani.
[taní]

What is your address (location)?
Cila është adresa juaj?
[tsíla əʃtə adrésa júaj?]

My address is …
Adresa ime është …
[adrésa imɛ əʃtə …]

Your destination?
Destinacioni juaj?
[dɛstinatsióni júaj?]

Excuse me, …
Më falni, …
[mə fálni, …]

Are you available?
Jeni i lirë?
[jéni i lírə?]

How much is it to get to …?
Sa kushton deri në …?
[sa kuʃtón déri nə …?]

Do you know where it is?
E dini ku ndodhet?
[ɛ díni ku ndóðɛt?]

Airport, please.
Në aeroport, ju lutem.
[nə aɛropórt], [ju lútɛm]

Stop here, please.
Ju lutem, ndaloni këtu.
[ju lútɛm], [ndalóni kətú]

It's not here.
Nuk është këtu.
[nuk əʃtə kətú]

This is the wrong address.
Kjo është adresë e gabuar.
[kjo əʃtə adrésə ɛ gabúar]

Turn left.
Kthehuni majtas.
[kθéhuni májtas]

Turn right.
Kthehuni djathtas.
[kθéhuni djáθtas]

How much do I owe you?	**Sa ju detyrohem?** [sa ju dɛtyróhɛm?]
I'd like a receipt, please.	**Ju lutem, më jepni një faturë.** [ju lútɛm], [mə jépni ɲə fatúrə]
Keep the change.	**Mbajeni kusurin.** [mbájɛni kusúrin]

Would you please wait for me?	**Mund të më prisni, ju lutem?** [mund tə mə prísni], [ju lútɛm?]
five minutes	**pesë minuta** [pésə minúta]
ten minutes	**dhjetë minuta** [ðjétə minúta]
fifteen minutes	**pesëmbëdhjetë minuta** [pɛsəmbəðjétə minúta]
twenty minutes	**njëzet minuta** [ɲəzét minúta]
half an hour	**gjysmë ore** [ɟýsmə órɛ]

Hotel

Hello.	**Përshëndetje.** [pərʃəndétjɛ]
My name is ...	**Më quajnë ...** [mə cúajnə ...]
I have a reservation.	**Kam një rezervim.** [kam ɲə rɛzɛrvím]
I need ...	**Më nevojitet ...** [mə nɛvojítɛt ...]
a single room	**dhomë teke** [ðómə tékɛ]
a double room	**dhomë dyshe** [ðómə dýʃɛ]
How much is that?	**Sa kushton?** [sa kuʃtón?]
That's a bit expensive.	**Është pak shtrenjtë.** [əʃtə pak ʃtréɲtə]
Do you have anything else?	**Keni ndonjë gjë tjetër?** [kéni ndóɲə ɟə tjétər?]
I'll take it.	**Do ta marr.** [do ta mar]
I'll pay in cash.	**Do paguaj me para në dorë.** [do pagúaj mɛ pará nə dórə]
I've got a problem.	**Kam një problem.** [kam ɲə problém]
My ... is broken.	**Më është prishur ...** [mə əʃtə príʃur ...]
My ... is out of order.	**Nuk funksionon ...** [nuk funksionón ...]
TV	**televizor** [tɛlɛvizór]
air conditioner	**kondicioner** [konditsionér]
tap	**çezma** [tʃézma]
shower	**dushi** [duʃi]
sink	**lavamani** [lavamáni]
safe	**kasaforta** [kasafórta]

door lock	**brava e derës** [bráva ɛ dérəs]
electrical outlet	**paneli elektrik** [panéli ɛlɛktrík]
hairdryer	**tharësja e flokëve** [θárəsja ɛ flókəvɛ]

I don't have ...	**Nuk kam ...** [nuk kam ...]
water	**ujë** [újə]
light	**drita** [dríta]
electricity	**korrent** [korént]

Can you give me ...?	**Mund të më jepni ...?** [mund tə mə jépni ...?]
a towel	**një peshqir** [ɲə pɛʃcír]
a blanket	**një çarçaf** [ɲə tʃartʃáf]
slippers	**shapka** [ʃápka]
a robe	**penuar** [pɛnuár]
shampoo	**shampo** [ʃampó]
soap	**sapun** [sapún]

I'd like to change rooms.	**Dua të ndryshoj dhomën.** [dúa tə ndryʃój ðómən]
I can't find my key.	**Nuk po gjej çelësin.** [nuk po ɟɛj tʃéləsin]
Could you open my room, please?	**Mund të më hapni derën, ju lutem?** [mund tə mə hápni dérən], [ju lútɛm?]
Who's there?	**Kush është?** [kuʃ éʃtə?]
Come in!	**Hyni!** [hýni!]
Just a minute!	**Një minutë!** [ɲə minútə!]
Not right now, please.	**Jo tani, ju lutem.** [jo taní], [ju lútɛm]

Come to my room, please.	**Ju lutem, ejani në dhomë.** [ju lútɛm], [éjani nə ðómə]
I'd like to order food service.	**Dua të porosisja ushqim.** [dúa tə porosísja uʃcím]
My room number is ...	**Numri i dhomës është ...** [númri i ðóməs éʃtə ...]

I'm leaving …	**Po largohem …** [po largóhɛm …]
We're leaving …	**Po largohemi …** [po largóhɛmi …]
right now	**tani** [taní]
this afternoon	**këtë pasdite** [kétə pasdítɛ]
tonight	**sonte** [sóntɛ]
tomorrow	**nesër** [nésər]
tomorrow morning	**nesër në mëngjes** [nésər nə mənɟés]
tomorrow evening	**nesër në mbrëmje** [nésər nə mbrémjɛ]
the day after tomorrow	**pasnesër** [pasnésər]

I'd like to pay.	**Dua të paguaj.** [dúa tə pagúaj]
Everything was wonderful.	**Gjithçka ishte e mrekullueshme.** [ɟíθtʃká íʃtɛ ɛ mrɛkuɫúɛʃmɛ]
Where can I get a taxi?	**Ku mund të gjej një taksi?** [ku mund tə ɟɛj ɲə táksi?]
Would you call a taxi for me, please?	**Mund të më thërrisni një taksi, ju lutem?** [mund tə mə θərísni ɲə táksi, ju lútɛm?]

Restaurant

Can I look at the menu, please?	**Mund të shoh menynë, ju lutem?** [mund tə ʃoh mɛnýnə], [ju lútɛm?]
Table for one.	**Tavolinë për një person.** [tavolínə pər ɲə pɛrsón]
There are two (three, four) of us.	**Jemi dy (tre, katër) vetë.** [jémi dy (trɛ], [kátər) vétə]

Smoking	**Lejohet duhani** [lɛjóhɛt duháni]
No smoking	**Ndalohet duhani** [ndalóhɛt duháni]
Excuse me! (addressing a waiter)	**Më falni!** [mə fálni!]
menu	**menyja** [mɛnýja]
wine list	**menyja e verave** [mɛnýja ɛ vɛravɛ]
The menu, please.	**Menynë, ju lutem.** [mɛnýnə], [ju lútɛm]

Are you ready to order?	**Jeni gati për të dhënë porosinë?** [jéni gáti pər tə ðénə porosínə?]
What will you have?	**Çfarë do të merrni?** [tʃfárə do tə mérni?]
I'll have ...	**Do të marr ...** [do tə mar ...]

I'm a vegetarian.	**Jam vegjetarian /vegjetariane/.** [jam vɛɟɛtarián /vɛɟɛtariánɛ/]
meat	**mish** [miʃ]
fish	**peshk** [pɛʃk]
vegetables	**perime** [pɛrímɛ]
Do you have vegetarian dishes?	**Keni gatime për vegjetarianë?** [kéni gatímɛ pər vɛɟɛtariánə?]
I don't eat pork.	**Nuk ha mish derri.** [nuk ha miʃ déri]
Band-Aid	**Ai /Ajo/ nuk ha mish.** [aí /ajó/ nuk ha miʃ]
I am allergic to ...	**Kam alergji nga ...** [kam alɛrɟí ŋa ...]

Would you please bring me … | **Mund të më sillni …**
[mund tə mə síłni …]

salt | pepper | sugar | **kripë | piper | sheqer**
[krípə | pipér | ʃɛcér]

coffee | tea | dessert | **kafe | çaj | ëmbëlsirë**
[káfɛ | tʃaj | əmbəlsírə]

water | sparkling | plain | **ujë | me gaz | pa gaz**
[újə | mɛ gaz | pa gaz]

a spoon | fork | knife | **një lugë | pirun | thikë**
[ɲə lúgə | pirún | θíkə]

a plate | napkin | **një pjatë | pecetë**
[ɲə pjátə | pɛtsétə]

Enjoy your meal! | **Ju bëftë mirë!**
[ju bə́ftə mírə!]

One more, please. | **Dhe një tjetër, ju lutem.**
[ðɛ ɲə tjétər], [ju lútɛm]

It was very delicious. | **ishte shumë e shijshme.**
[íʃtɛ ʃúmə ɛ ʃíjʃmɛ]

check | change | tip | **llogari | kusur | bakshish**
[łogarí | kusúr | bakʃíʃ]

Check, please.
(Could I have the check, please?) | **Llogarinë, ju lutem.**
[łogarínə], [ju lútɛm]

Can I pay by credit card? | **Mund të paguaj me kartelë krediti?**
[mund tə pagúaj mɛ kartélə krɛdíti?]

I'm sorry, there's a mistake here. | **Më falni por ka një gabim këtu.**
[mə fálni por ka ɲə gabím kətú]

Shopping

Can I help you?	**Mund t'ju ndihmoj?** [mund t'ju ndihmój?]
Do you have ...?	**Keni ...?** [kéni ...?]
I'm looking for ...	**Kërkoj ...** [kərkój ...]
I need ...	**Më nevojitet ...** [mə nɛvojítɛt ...]

I'm just looking.	**Thjesht po shoh.** [θjɛʃt po ʃoh]
We're just looking.	**Thjesht po shohim.** [θjɛʃt po ʃóhim]
I'll come back later.	**Do vij më vonë.** [do víj mə vónə]
We'll come back later.	**Do vijmë më vonë.** [do víjmə mə vónə]
discounts | sale	**ulje çmimesh | ulje** [úljɛ t͡ʃmímɛʃ | úljɛ]

Would you please show me ...	**Ju lutem mund të më tregoni ...** [ju lútɛm mund tə mə trɛgóni ...]
Would you please give me ...	**Ju lutem mund të më jepni ...** [ju lútɛm mund tə mə jépni ...]
Can I try it on?	**Mund ta provoj?** [mund ta provój?]
Excuse me, where's the fitting room?	**Më falni, ku është dhoma e provës?** [mə fálni], [ku əʃtə ðóma ɛ próvəs?]
Which color would you like?	**Çfarë ngjyre e doni?** [t͡ʃfárə nɟýrɛ ɛ dóni?]
size | length	**numri | gjatësia** [númri | ɟatəsía]
How does it fit?	**Si ju rri?** [si ju ri?]

How much is it?	**Sa kushton?** [sa kuʃtón?]
That's too expensive.	**Është shumë shtrenjtë.** [əʃtə ʃúmə ʃtrénjtə]
I'll take it.	**Do ta marr.** [do ta mar]
Excuse me, where do I pay?	**Më falni, ku duhet të paguaj?** [mə fálni], [ku dúhɛt tə pagúaj?]

Will you pay in cash or credit card?

Do paguani me para në dorë apo kartelë krediti?
[do pagúani mɛ pará nə dórə apo kartélə krɛdíti?]

In cash | with credit card

Me para në dorë | me kartelë krediti
[mɛ pará nə dórə | mɛ kartélə krɛdíti]

Do you want the receipt?

Dëshironi faturën?
[dəʃiróni fatúrən?]

Yes, please.

Po faleminderit.
[po falɛmindérit]

No, it's OK.

Jo, s'ka problem.
[jo], [s'ka problém]

Thank you. Have a nice day!

Faleminderit. Ditë të mbarë!
[falɛmindérit. dítə tə mbárə!]

In town

Excuse me, ...	**Më falni, ju lutem.**
	[mə fálni], [ju lútɛm]
I'm looking for ...	**Kërkoj ...**
	[kərkój ...]
the subway	**metronë**
	[mɛtrónə]
my hotel	**hotelin**
	[hotélin]
the movie theater	**kinemanë**
	[kinɛmánə]
a taxi stand	**një stacion për taksi**
	[ɲə statsión pər táksi]

an ATM	**një bankomat**
	[ɲə bankomát]
a foreign exchange office	**një zyrë shkëmbimi parash**
	[ɲə zýrə ʃkəmbími paráʃ]
an internet café	**një internet kafe**
	[ɲə intɛrnét káfɛ]
... street	**rrugën ...**
	[rúgən ...]
this place	**këtë vend**
	[kétə vɛnd]

Do you know where ... is?	**Dini ku ndodhet ...?**
	[díni ku ndóðɛt ...?]
Which street is this?	**Cila rrugë është kjo?**
	[tsíla rúgə éʃtə kjó?]
Show me where we are right now.	**Më tregoni ku ndodhemi tani.**
	[mə trɛgóni ku ndóðɛmi taní]
Can I get there on foot?	**Mund të shkoj me këmbë deri atje?**
	[mund tə ʃkoj mɛ kémbə déri atjé?]
Do you have a map of the city?	**Keni hartë të qytetit?**
	[kéni hártə tə cytétit?]

How much is a ticket to get in?	**Sa kushton një biletë hyrje?**
	[sa kuʃtón ɲə bilétə hýrjɛ?]
Can I take pictures here?	**Mund të bëj fotografi këtu?**
	[mund tə bəj fotografí kətú?]
Are you open?	**Jeni të hapur?**
	[jéni tə hápur?]

When do you open?

Kur hapeni?
[kur hápɛni?]

When do you close?

Kur mbylleni?
[kur mbýɫɛni?]

Money

money	**para** [pará]
cash	**para në dorë** [pará nə dórə]
paper money	**kartëmonedha** [kartəmonéða]
loose change	**kusur** [kusúr]
check | change | tip	**llogari | kusur | bakshish** [ɫogarí | kusúr | bakʃíʃ]

credit card	**kartelë krediti** [kartélə krɛdíti]
wallet	**portofol** [portofól]
to buy	**të blej** [tə blɛj]
to pay	**të paguaj** [tə pagúaj]
fine	**gjobë** [ɟóbə]
free	**falas** [fálas]

Where can I buy ...?	**Ku mund të blej ...?** [ku mund tə bléj ...?]
Is the bank open now?	**Është banka e hapur tani?** [éʃtə bánka ɛ hápur taní?]
When does it open?	**Kur hapet?** [kur hápɛt?]
When does it close?	**Kur mbyllet?** [kur mbýɫɛt?]

How much?	**Sa kushton?** [sa kuʃtón?]
How much is this?	**Sa kushton kjo?** [sa kuʃtón kjo?]
That's too expensive.	**Është shumë shtrenjtë.** [éʃtə ʃúmə ʃtréɲtə]

Excuse me, where do I pay?	**Më falni, ku duhet të paguaj?** [mə fálni], [ku dúhɛt tə pagúaj?]
Check, please.	**Llogarinë, ju lutem.** [ɫogarínə], [ju lútɛm]

Can I pay by credit card? **Mund të paguaj me kartelë krediti?**
[mund tə pagúaj mɛ kartélə krɛdíti?]

Is there an ATM here? **Ka ndonjë bankomat këtu?**
[ka ndóɲə bankomát kətú?]

I'm looking for an ATM. **Kërkoj një bankomat.**
[kərkój ɲə bankomát]

I'm looking for a foreign exchange office. **Kërkoj një zyrë të këmbimit valutor.**
[kərkój ɲə zýrə tə kəmbímit valutór]

I'd like to change … **Dua të këmbej …**
[dúa tə kəmbéj …]

What is the exchange rate? **Sa është kursi i këmbimit?**
[sa éʃtə kúrsi i kəmbímit?]

Do you need my passport? **Ju duhet pasaporta ime?**
[ju dúhɛt pasapórta ímɛ?]

Time

What time is it?	**Sa është ora?** [sa ə́ʃtə óra?]
When?	**Kur?** [kur?]
At what time?	**Në çfarë ore?** [nə tʃfárə órɛ?]
now | later | after ...	**tani | më vonë | pas ...** [taní | mə vónə | pas ...]

one o'clock	**ora një** [óra ɲə]
one fifteen	**një e çerek** [ɲə ɛ tʃɛrék]
one thirty	**një e tridhjetë** [ɲə ɛ triðjétə]
one forty-five	**një e dyzet e pesë** [ɲə ɛ dyzét ɛ pésə]

one | two | three	**një | dy | tre** [ɲə | dy | trɛ]
four | five | six	**katër | pesë | gjashtë** [kátər | pésə | ɟáʃtə]
seven | eight | nine	**shtatë | tetë | nëntë** [ʃtátə | tétə | nə́ntə]
ten | eleven | twelve	**dhjetë | njëmbëdhjetë | dymbëdhjetë** [ðjétə | ɲəmbəðjétə | dymbəðjétə]

in ...	**për ...** [pər ...]
five minutes	**pesë minuta** [pésə minúta]
ten minutes	**dhjetë minuta** [ðjétə minúta]
fifteen minutes	**pesëmbëdhjetë minuta** [pɛsəmbəðjétə minúta]
twenty minutes	**njëzet minuta** [ɲəzét minúta]
half an hour	**gjysmë ore** [ɟýsmə órɛ]
an hour	**një orë** [ɲə órə]

in the morning	**në mëngjes** [nə mənɟés]
early in the morning	**në mëngjes herët** [nə mənɟés hérət]
this morning	**sot në mëngjes** [sot nə mənɟés]
tomorrow morning	**nesër në mëngjes** [nésər nə mənɟés]

in the middle of the day	**në mesditë** [nə mɛsdítə]
in the afternoon	**në pasdite** [nə pasdítɛ]
in the evening	**në mbrëmje** [nə mbrə́mjɛ]
tonight	**sonte** [sóntɛ]

at night	**natën** [nátən]
yesterday	**dje** [djé]
today	**sot** [sot]
tomorrow	**nesër** [nésər]
the day after tomorrow	**pasnesër** [pasnésər]

What day is it today?	**Çfarë dite është sot?** [tʃfárə dítɛ ə́ʃtə sot?]
It's …	**Është …** [ə́ʃtə …]
Monday	**E hënë** [ɛ hə́nə]
Tuesday	**E martë** [ɛ mártə]
Wednesday	**E mërkurë** [ɛ mərkúrə]

Thursday	**E enjte** [ɛ éɲtɛ]
Friday	**E premte** [ɛ prémtɛ]
Saturday	**E shtunë** [ɛ ʃtúnə]
Sunday	**E diel** [ɛ díɛl]

Greetings. Introductions

Hello.	**Përshëndetje.** [pərʃəndétjɛ]
Pleased to meet you.	**Kënaqësi që u njohëm.** [kənacəsí cə u ɲóhəm]
Me too.	**Gjithashtu.** [ɟiθaʃtú]
I'd like you to meet ...	**Ju prezantoj me ...** [ju prɛzantój mɛ ...]
Nice to meet you.	**Gëzohem që u njohëm.** [gəzóhɛm cə u ɲóhəm]

How are you?	**Si jeni?** [si jéni?]
My name is ...	**Më quajnë ...** [mə cúajnə ...]
His name is ...	**Ai quhet ...** [ai cúhɛt ...]
Her name is ...	**Ajo quhet ...** [ajó cúhɛt ...]
What's your name?	**Si quheni?** [si cúhɛni?]
What's his name?	**Si e quajnë?** [si ɛ cúajnə?]
What's her name?	**Si e quajnë?** [si ɛ cúajnə?]

What's your last name?	**Si e keni mbiemrin?** [si ɛ kéni mbiémrin?]
You can call me ...	**Mund të më thërrisni ...** [mund tə mə θərísni ...]
Where are you from?	**Nga jeni?** [ŋa jéni?]
I'm from ...	**Jam nga ...** [jam ŋa ...]
What do you do for a living?	**Me çfarë merreni?** [mɛ tʃfárə mérɛni?]

Who is this?	**Kush është ky?** [kuʃ əʃtə ky?]
Who is he?	**Kush është ai?** [kuʃ əʃtə ái?]

Who is she?	**Kush është ajo?** [kuʃ əʃtə ajó?]
Who are they?	**Kush janë ata?** [kuʃ jánə atá?]

This is …	**Ky /Kjo/ është …** [ky /kjo/ éʃtə …]
my friend (masc.)	**shoku im** [ʃóku im]
my friend (fem.)	**shoqja ime** [ʃócja ímɛ]
my husband	**bashkëshorti im** [baʃkəʃórti im]
my wife	**bashkëshortja ime** [baʃkəʃórtja imɛ]

my father	**babai im** [babái im]
my mother	**nëna ime** [nóna ímɛ]
my brother	**vëllai im** [vəɫái im]
my sister	**motra ime** [mótra ímɛ]
my son	**djali im** [djáli im]
my daughter	**vajza ime** [vájza ímɛ]

This is our son.	**Ky është djali ynë.** [ky éʃtə djáli ýnə]
This is our daughter.	**Kjo është vajza jonë.** [kjo éʃtə vájza jónə]
These are my children.	**Këta janë fëmijët e mi.** [kətá jánə fəmíjət ɛ mi]
These are our children.	**Këta janë fëmijët tanë.** [kətá jánə fəmíjət tánə]

Farewells

Good bye!	**Mirupafshim!** [mirupáfʃim!]
Bye! (inform.)	**Pafshim!** [páfʃim!]
See you tomorrow.	**Shihemi nesër.** [ʃíhɛmi nésər]
See you soon.	**Shihemi së shpejti.** [ʃíhɛmi sə ʃpéjti]
See you at seven.	**Shihemi në orën shtatë.** [ʃíhɛmi nə órən ʃtátə]

Have fun!	**ia kalofshi mirë!** [ía kalófʃi mírə!]
Talk to you later.	**Flasim më vonë.** [flásim mə vónə]
Have a nice weekend.	**Fundjavë të këndshme.** [fundjávə tə kéndʃmɛ]
Good night.	**Natën e mirë.** [nátən ɛ mírə]

It's time for me to go.	**erdhi koha të ik.** [érði kóha tə ik]
I have to go.	**Duhet të ik.** [dúhɛt tə ik]
I will be right back.	**Kthehem menjëherë.** [kθéhɛm mɛɲəhérə]

It's late.	**Është vonë.** [éʃtə vónə]
I have to get up early.	**Duhet të ngrihem herët.** [dúhɛt tə ɲríhɛm hérət]
I'm leaving tomorrow.	**Do ik nesër.** [do ik nésər]
We're leaving tomorrow.	**Do ikim nesër.** [do íkim nésər]

Have a nice trip!	**Udhëtim të mbarë!** [uðətím tə mbárə!]
It was nice meeting you.	**ishte kënaqësi.** [íʃtɛ kənacəsí]
It was nice talking to you.	**ishte kënaqësi që folëm.** [íʃtɛ kənacəsí cə fóləm]
Thanks for everything.	**Faleminderit për gjithçka.** [falɛmindérit pər ɟíθtʃka]

I had a very good time.

ia kalova shumë mirë.
[ía kalóva ʃúmə mírə]

We had a very good time.

ia kaluam shumë mirë.
[ía kalúam ʃúmə mírə]

It was really great.

ishte vërtet fantastike.
[íʃtɛ vərtét fantastíkɛ]

I'm going to miss you.

Do më marrë malli.
[do mə márə máɫi]

We're going to miss you.

Do na marrë malli.
[do na márə máɫi]

Good luck!

Suksese!
[suksésɛ!]

Say hi to ...

I bën të fala ...
[i bən tə fála ...]

Foreign language

I don't understand.	**Nuk kuptoj.** [nuk kuptój]
Write it down, please.	**Shkruajeni, ju lutem.** [ʃkrúajɛni], [ju lútɛm]
Do you speak ...?	**Flisni ...?** [flísni ...?]

I speak a little bit of ...	**Flas pak ...** [flás pak ...]
English	**Anglisht** [aɲlíʃt]
Turkish	**Turqisht** [turcíʃt]
Arabic	**Arabisht** [arabíʃt]
French	**Frëngjisht** [frəɲɟíʃt]

German	**Gjermanisht** [ɟɛrmaníʃt]
Italian	**Italisht** [italíʃt]
Spanish	**Spanjisht** [spaɲíʃt]
Portuguese	**Portugalisht** [portugalíʃt]
Chinese	**Kinezisht** [kinɛzíʃt]
Japanese	**Japonisht** [japoníʃt]

Can you repeat that, please.	**Mund ta përsërisni, ju lutem.** [mund ta pərsərísni], [ju lútɛm]
I understand.	**Kuptoj.** [kuptój]
I don't understand.	**Nuk kuptoj.** [nuk kuptój]
Please speak more slowly.	**Ju lutem, flisni më ngadalë.** [ju lútɛm], [flísni mə ŋadálə]

Is that correct? (Am I saying it right?)	**E saktë?** [ɛ sáktə?]
What is this? (What does this mean?)	**Çfarë është kjo?** [tʃfárə éʃtə kjó?]

47

Apologies

Excuse me, please.	**Më falni.**
	[mə fálni]
I'm sorry.	**Më vjen keq.**
	[mə vjɛn kɛc]
I'm really sorry.	**Më vjen shumë keq.**
	[mə vjɛn ʃúmə kɛc]
Sorry, it's my fault.	**Më fal, është faji im.**
	[mə fal], [əʃtə fáji im]
My mistake.	**Gabimi im.**
	[gabími im]

May I ...?	**Mund të ...?**
	[mund tə ...?]
Do you mind if I ...?	**Ju vjen keq nëse ...?**
	[ju vjɛn kɛc nésɛ ...?]
It's OK.	**Është në rregull.**
	[əʃtə nə réguɫ]
It's all right.	**Është në rregull.**
	[əʃtə nə réguɫ]
Don't worry about it.	**Mos u shqetësoni.**
	[mos u ʃcɛtəsóni]

Agreement

Yes.	**Po.**
	[po]
Yes, sure.	**Po, sigurisht,**
	[po], [siguríʃt]
OK (Good!)	**Në rregull.**
	[nə réguɫ]
Very well.	**Shumë mirë.**
	[ʃúmə mírə]
Certainly!	**Sigurisht!**
	[siguríʃt!]
I agree.	**Jam dakord.**
	[jam dakórd]

That's correct.	**E saktë.**
	[ɛ sáktə]
That's right.	**E drejtë.**
	[ɛ dréjtə]
You're right.	**Keni të drejtë.**
	[kéni tə dréjtə]
I don't mind.	**S'e kam problem.**
	[s'ɛ kam problém]
Absolutely right.	**Absolutisht e drejtë.**
	[absolutíʃt ɛ dréjtə]

It's possible.	**Është e mundur.**
	[ə́ʃtə ɛ múndur]
That's a good idea.	**Ide e mirë.**
	[idé ɛ mírə]
I can't say no.	**Nuk them dot jo.**
	[nuk θɛm dot jo]
I'd be happy to.	**Është kënaqësi.**
	[ə́ʃtə kənacəsí]
With pleasure.	**Me kënaqësi.**
	[mɛ kənacəsí]

Refusal. Expressing doubt

No.	**Jo.** [jo]
Certainly not.	**Sigurisht që jo.** [siguríʃt cə jo]
I don't agree.	**Nuk jam dakord.** [nuk jam dakórd]
I don't think so.	**Nuk ma ha mendja.** [nuk ma ha méndja]
It's not true.	**Nuk është e vërtetë.** [nuk éʃtə ɛ vərtétə]
You are wrong.	**E keni gabim.** [ɛ kéni gabím]
I think you are wrong.	**Më duket se e keni gabim.** [mə dúkɛt sɛ ɛ kéni gabím]
I'm not sure.	**Nuk jam i sigurt.** [nuk jam i sígurt]
It's impossible.	**Është e pamundur.** [éʃtə ɛ pámundur]
Nothing of the kind (sort)!	**Asgjë e këtij lloji!** [asɉə ɛ kətíj ɫóji!]
The exact opposite.	**Krejt e kundërta.** [kréjt ɛ kúndərta]
I'm against it.	**Jam kundër.** [jam kúndər]
I don't care.	**Nuk më intereson.** [nuk mə intɛrɛsón]
I have no idea.	**Nuk e kam idenë.** [nuk ɛ kam idénə]
I doubt it.	**Dyshoj.** [dyʃój]
Sorry, I can't.	**Më falni, nuk mundem.** [mə fálni], [nuk múndɛm]
Sorry, I don't want to.	**Më vjen keq, nuk dua.** [mə vjɛn kɛc], [nuk dúa]
Thank you, but I don't need this.	**Faleminderit, por s'kam nevojë për këtë.** [falɛmindérit], [por s'kam nɛvójə pər kəté]

It's getting late.

Po shkon vonë.
[po ʃkon vónə]

I have to get up early.

Duhet të ngrihem herët.
[dúhɛt tə ŋríhɛm hérət]

I don't feel well.

Nuk ndihem mirë.
[nuk ndíhɛm mírə]

Expressing gratitude

Thank you.	**Faleminderit.**
	[falɛmindérit]
Thank you very much.	**Faleminderit shumë.**
	[falɛmindérit ʃúmə]
I really appreciate it.	**E vlerësoj shumë.**
	[ɛ vlɛrəsój ʃúmə]
I'm really grateful to you.	**Ju jam shumë mirënjohës.**
	[ju jam ʃúmə mirəɲóhəs]
We are really grateful to you.	**Ju jemi shumë mirënjohës.**
	[ju jémi ʃúmə mirəɲóhəs]
Thank you for your time.	**Faleminderit për kohën që më kushtuat.**
	[falɛmindérit pər kóhən cə mə kuʃtúat]
Thanks for everything.	**Faleminderit për gjithçka.**
	[falɛmindérit pər ɟíθtʃka]
Thank you for ...	**Faleminderit për ...**
	[falɛmindérit pər ...]
your help	**ndihmën tuaj**
	[ndíhmən túaj]
a nice time	**kohën e këndshme**
	[kóhən ɛ kə́ndʃmɛ]
a wonderful meal	**një vakt i mrekullueshëm**
	[ɲə vakt i mrɛkułúɛʃəm]
a pleasant evening	**një mbrëmje e këndshme**
	[ɲə mbrə́mjɛ ɛ kə́ndʃmɛ]
a wonderful day	**një ditë e mrekullueshme**
	[ɲə dítə ɛ mrɛkułúɛʃmɛ]
an amazing journey	**një udhëtim i mahnitshëm**
	[ɲə uðətím i mahnítʃəm]
Don't mention it.	**Mos u shqetësoni fare.**
	[mos u ʃcɛtəsóni fárɛ]
You are welcome.	**Ju lutem.**
	[ju lútɛm]
Any time.	**Në çdo kohë.**
	[nə tʃdo kóhə]
My pleasure.	**Kënaqësia ime.**
	[kənacəsía ímɛ]

Forget it.

Harroje.
[harójɛ]

Don't worry about it.

Mos u shqetësoni.
[mos u ʃcɛtəsóni]

Congratulations. Best wishes

Congratulations! **Urime!**
[urímɛ!]

Happy birthday! **Gëzuar ditëlindjen!**
[gəzúar ditəlíndjɛn!]

Merry Christmas! **Gëzuar Krishtlindjet!**
[gəzúar kriʃtlíndjɛt!]

Happy New Year! **Gëzuar Vitin e Ri!**
[gəzúar vítin ɛ ri!]

Happy Easter! **Gëzuar Pashkët!**
[gəzúar páʃkət!]

Happy Hanukkah! **Gëzuar Hanukkah!**
[gəzúar hanúkkah!]

I'd like to propose a toast. **Dua të ngre një dolli.**
[dúa tə ŋré ɲə dotɬí]

Cheers! **Gëzuar!**
[gəzúar!]

Let's drink to ...! **Le të pijmë në shëndetin e ...!**
[lɛ tə píjmə nə ʃəndétin ɛ ...!]

To our success! **Për suksesin tonë!**
[pər suksésin tónə!]

To your success! **Për suksesin tuaj!**
[pər suksésin túaj!]

Good luck! **Suksese!**
[suksésɛ!]

Have a nice day! **Uroj një ditë të mbarë!**
[urój ɲə dítə tə mbárə!]

Have a good holiday! **Uroj pushime të këndshme!**
[urój puʃímɛ tə kəndʃmɛ!]

Have a safe journey! **Udhëtim të mbarë!**
[uðətím tə mbárə!]

I hope you get better soon! **Ju dëshiroj shërim të shpejtë!**
[ju dəʃirój ʃərím tə ʃpéjtə!]

Socializing

Why are you sad?	**Pse jeni i /e/ mërzitur?** [psɛ jéni i /ɛ/ mərzítur?]
Smile! Cheer up!	**Buzëqeshni! Gëzohuni!** [buzəcéʃni! gəzóhuni!]
Are you free tonight?	**Je i /e/ lirë sonte?** [jɛ i /ɛ/ lírə sóntɛ?]

May I offer you a drink?	**Mund t'ju ofroj një pije?** [mund t'ju ofrój ɲə píjɛ?]
Would you like to dance?	**Doni të kërcejmë?** [dóni tə kərtséjmə?]
Let's go to the movies.	**Shkojmë në kinema.** [ʃkójmə nə kinɛmá]

May I invite you to ...?	**Mund t'ju ftoj ...?** [mund t'ju ftoj ...?]
a restaurant	**në restorant** [nə rɛstoránt]
the movies	**në kinema** [nə kinɛmá]
the theater	**në teatër** [nə tɛátər]
go for a walk	**për një shëtitje** [pər ɲə ʃətítjɛ]

At what time?	**Në çfarë ore?** [nə tʃfárə órɛ?]
tonight	**sonte** [sóntɛ]
at six	**në gjashtë** [nə ɟáʃtə]
at seven	**në shtatë** [nə ʃtátə]
at eight	**në tetë** [nə tétə]
at nine	**në nëntë** [nə nɛ́ntə]

Do you like it here?	**Ju pëlqen këtu?** [ju pəlcén kətú?]
Are you here with someone?	**Keni ardhur të shoqëruar?** [kéni árður tə ʃocərúar?]
I'm with my friend.	**Jam me një shok /shoqe/.** [jam mɛ ɲə ʃok /ʃócɛ/]

I'm with my friends.

Jam me shoqëri.
[jam mɛ ʃocərí]

No, I'm alone.

Jo, jam vetëm.
[jo], [jam vétəm]

Do you have a boyfriend?

Ke të dashur?
[kɛ tə dáʃur?]

I have a boyfriend.

Kam të dashur.
[kam tə dáʃur]

Do you have a girlfriend?

Ke të dashur?
[kɛ tə dáʃur?]

I have a girlfriend.

Kam të dashur.
[kam tə dáʃur]

Can I see you again?

Mund të takohemi përsëri?
[mund tə takóhɛmi pərsərí?]

Can I call you?

Mund të të telefonoj?
[mund tə tə tɛlɛfonój?]

Call me. (Give me a call.)

Më telefono.
[mə tɛlɛfonó]

What's your number?

Cili është numri yt?
[tsíli ə́ʃtə númri yt?]

I miss you.

Më mungon.
[mə muŋón]

You have a beautiful name.

Keni emër të bukur.
[kéni émər tə búkur]

I love you.

Të dua.
[tə dúa]

Will you marry me?

Do martohesh me mua?
[do martóhɛʃ mɛ múa?]

You're kidding!

Bëni shaka!
[bəni ʃaká!]

I'm just kidding.

Bëj shaka.
[bəj ʃaká]

Are you serious?

E keni seriozisht?
[ɛ kéni sɛriozíʃt?]

I'm serious.

E kam seriozisht.
[ɛ kam sɛriozíʃt]

Really?!

Vërtet?!
[vərtét?!]

It's unbelievable!

E pabesueshme!
[ɛ pabɛsúeʃmɛ!]

I don't believe you.

S'ju besoj.
[s'ju bɛsój]

I can't.

S'mundem.
[s'múndɛm]

I don't know.

Nuk e di.
[nuk ɛ di]

I don't understand you.

Nuk ju kuptoj.
[nuk ju kuptój]

Please go away.	**Ju lutem largohuni.**
	[ju lútɛm largóhuni]
Leave me alone!	**Më lini të qetë!**
	[mə líni tə cétə!]

I can't stand him.	**Se duroj dot.**
	[sɛ durój dot]
You are disgusting!	**Jeni të neveritshëm!**
	[jéni tə nɛvɛrítʃəm!]
I'll call the police!	**Do thërras policinë!**
	[do θərás politsínə!]

Sharing impressions. Emotions

I like it.	**Më pëlqen.** [mə pəlcén]
Very nice.	**Shumë bukur** [ʃúmə búkur]
That's great!	**Fantastike!** [fantastíkɛ!]
It's not bad.	**Nuk është keq.** [nuk əʃtə kɛc]
I don't like it.	**Nuk më pëlqen.** [nuk mə pəlcén]
It's not good.	**Nuk është mirë.** [nuk əʃtə mírə]
It's bad.	**Është keq.** [əʃtə kɛc]
It's very bad.	**Është shumë keq.** [əʃtə ʃúmə kɛc]
It's disgusting.	**Është e shpifur.** [əʃtə ɛ ʃpífur]
I'm happy.	**Jam i /e/ lumtur.** [jam i /ɛ/ lúmtur]
I'm content.	**Jam i /e/ kënaqur.** [jam i /ɛ/ kənácur]
I'm in love.	**Jam i /e/ dashuruar.** [jam i /ɛ/ daʃurúar]
I'm calm.	**Jam i /e/ qetë.** [jam i /ɛ/ cétə]
I'm bored.	**Jam i /e/ mërzitur.** [jam i /ɛ/ mərzítur]
I'm tired.	**Jam i /e/ lodhur.** [jam i /ɛ/ lóður]
I'm sad.	**Jam i /e/ trishtuar.** [jam i /ɛ/ triʃtúar]
I'm frightened.	**Jam i /e/ frikësuar.** [jam i /ɛ/ frikəsúar]
I'm angry.	**Jam i /e/ zemëruar.** [jam i /ɛ/ zɛmərúar]
I'm worried.	**Jam i /e/ shqetësuar.** [jam i /ɛ/ ʃcɛtəsúar]
I'm nervous.	**Jam nervoz /nervoze/.** [jam nɛrvóz /nɛrvózɛ/]

I'm jealous. (envious)   **Jam xheloz /xheloze/.**
[jam dʒɛlóz /dʒɛlózɛ/]

I'm surprised.   **Jam i /e/ befasuar.**
[jam i /ɛ/ bɛfasúar]

I'm perplexed.   **Jam i /e/ hutuar.**
[jam i /ɛ/ hutúar]

Problems. Accidents

I've got a problem.	**Kam një problem.**
	[kam ɲə problém]
We've got a problem.	**Kemi një problem.**
	[kémi ɲə problém]
I'm lost.	**Kam humbur.**
	[kam húmbur]
I missed the last bus (train).	**Humba autobusin e fundit.**
	[húmba autobúsin ɛ fúndit]
I don't have any money left.	**Kam mbetur pa para.**
	[kam mbétur pa pará]

I've lost my ...	**Humba ...**
	[húmba ...]
Someone stole my ...	**Dikush më vodhi ...**
	[dikúʃ mə vóði ...]
passport	**pasaportën**
	[pasapórtən]
wallet	**portofol**
	[portofól]
papers	**dokumentet**
	[dokuméntɛt]
ticket	**biletën**
	[bilétən]
money	**para**
	[pará]
handbag	**çantën**
	[tʃántən]
camera	**aparatin fotografik**
	[aparátin fotografík]
laptop	**laptop**
	[laptóp]
tablet computer	**kompjuterin tabletë**
	[kompjutérin tablétə]
mobile phone	**celularin**
	[tsɛlulárin]

Help me!	**Ndihmë!**
	[ndíhmə!]
What's happened?	**Çfarë ndodhi?**
	[tʃfárə ndóði?]
fire	**zjarr**
	[zjar]
shooting	**të shtëna**
	[tə ʃténa]

murder	**vrasje** [vrásjɛ]
explosion	**shpërthim** [ʃpərθím]
fight	**përleshje** [pərléʃjɛ]

Call the police!	**Thërrisni policinë!** [θərísni politsínə!]
Please hurry up!	**Ju lutem nxitoni!** [ju lútɛm ndzitóni!]
I'm looking for the police station.	**Kërkoj komisariatin e policisë.** [kərkój komisariátin ɛ politsísə]
I need to make a call.	**Duhet të bëj një telefonatë.** [dúhɛt tə bəj ɲə tɛlɛfonátə]
May I use your phone?	**Mund të përdor telefonin tuaj?** [mund tə pərdór tɛlɛfónin túaj?]

I've been …	**Më …** [mə …]
mugged	**sulmuan** [sulmúan]
robbed	**grabitën** [grabítən]
raped	**përdhunuan** [pərðunúan]
attacked (beaten up)	**rrahën** [ráhən]

Are you all right?	**Jeni mirë?** [jéni mírə?]
Did you see who it was?	**E patë kush ishte?** [ɛ pátə kuʃ íʃtɛ?]
Would you be able to recognize the person?	**Mund ta identifikoni personin?** [mund ta idɛntifikóni pɛrsónin?]
Are you sure?	**Jeni i /e/ sigurt?** [jéni i /ɛ/ sígurt?]

Please calm down.	**Ju lutem qetësohuni.** [ju lútɛm cɛtəsóhuni]
Take it easy!	**Merreni me qetësi!** [mérɛni mɛ cɛtəsí!]
Don't worry!	**Mos u shqetësoni!** [mos u ʃcɛtəsóni!]
Everything will be fine.	**Çdo gjë do rregullohet.** [tʃdo ɟə do rɛguɫóhɛt]
Everything's all right.	**Çdo gjë është në rregull.** [tʃdo ɟə éʃtə nə réguɫ]
Come here, please.	**ejani këtu, ju lutem.** [éjani kətú], [ju lútɛm]
I have some questions for you.	**Kam disa pyetje për ju.** [kam dísa pýɛtjɛ pər ju]

Wait a moment, please.

Prisni pak, ju lutem.
[prísni pak], [ju lútɛm]

Do you have any I.D.?

A keni ndonjë dokument identifikimi?
[a kéni ndóɲə dokumént idɛntifikími?]

Thanks. You can leave now.

Faleminderit. Mund të largoheni.
[falɛmindérit. mund tə largóhɛni.]

Hands behind your head!

Duart prapa kokës!
[dúart prápa kókəs!]

You're under arrest!

Jeni i /e/ arrestuar!
[jéni i /ɛ/ arɛstúar!]

Health problems

Please help me.	**Ju lutem më ndihmoni.** [ju lútɛm mə ndihmóni]
I don't feel well.	**Nuk ndihem mirë.** [nuk ndíhɛm mírə]
My husband doesn't feel well.	**Burri im nuk ndjehet mirë.** [búri im nuk ndjéhɛt mírə]
My son ...	**Djali im ...** [djáli im ...]
My father ...	**Babai im ...** [babái im ...]

My wife doesn't feel well.	**Gruaja ime nuk ndihet mirë.** [grúaja ímɛ nuk ndíhɛt mírə]
My daughter ...	**Vajza ime ...** [vájza ímɛ ...]
My mother ...	**Nëna ime ...** [néna ímɛ ...]

I've got a ...	**Kam ...** [kam ...]
headache	**dhimbje koke** [ðímbjɛ kókɛ]
sore throat	**dhimbje fyti** [ðímbjɛ fýti]
stomach ache	**dhimbje stomaku** [ðímbjɛ stomáku]
toothache	**dhimbje dhëmbi** [ðímbjɛ ðémbi]

I feel dizzy.	**Ndjehem i /e/ trullosur.** [ndjéhɛm i /ɛ/ truɫósur]
He has a fever.	**Ka ethe.** [ka éθɛ]
She has a fever.	**Ajo ka ethe.** [ajó ka éθɛ]
I can't breathe.	**Nuk marr dot frymë.** [nuk mar dot frýmə]

I'm short of breath.	**Mbeta pa frymë.** [mbéta pa frýmə]
I am asthmatic.	**unë jam astmatik.** [únə jam astmatík]
I am diabetic.	**Jam me diabet.** [jam mɛ diabét]

I can't sleep.

Nuk fle dot.
[nuk flɛ dot]

food poisoning

helmim nga ushqimi
[hɛlmím ŋa uʃcími]

It hurts here.

Më dhemb këtu.
[mə ðɛmb kətú]

Help me!

Ndihmë!
[ndíhmə!]

I am here!

Jam këtu!
[jam kətú!]

We are here!

Jemi këtu!
[jémi kətú!]

Get me out of here!

Më nxirrni nga këtu!
[mə ndzírni ŋa kətú!]

I need a doctor.

Kam nevojë për doktor.
[kam nɛvójə pər doktór]

I can't move.

Nuk lëviz dot.
[nuk ləvíz dot]

I can't move my legs.

Nuk lëviz dot këmbët.
[nuk ləvíz dot kémbət]

I have a wound.

Jam plagosur.
[jam plagósur]

Is it serious?

A është serioze?
[a éʃtə sɛriózɛ?]

My documents are in my pocket.

Dokumentet e mia janë në xhep.
[dokuméntɛt ɛ mía jánə nə dʒép]

Calm down!

Qetësohuni!
[cɛtəsóhuni!]

May I use your phone?

Mund të përdor telefonin tuaj?
[mund tə pərdór tɛlɛfónin túaj?]

Call an ambulance!

Thërrisni një ambulancë!
[θərísni ɲə ambulántsə!]

It's urgent!

Është urgjente!
[éʃtə urɟéntɛ!]

It's an emergency!

Është rast urgjent!
[éʃtə rast urɟént!]

Please hurry up!

Ju lutem nxitoni!
[ju lútɛm ndzitóni!]

Would you please call a doctor?

Mund të thërrisni një doktor, ju lutem?
[mund tə θərísni ɲə doktór], [ju lútɛm?]

Where is the hospital?

Ku është spitali?
[ku éʃtə spitáli?]

How are you feeling?

Si ndiheni?
[si ndíhɛni?]

Are you all right?

Jeni mirë?
[jéni mírə?]

What's happened?

Çfarë ndodhi?
[tʃfárə ndóði?]

I feel better now.

Ndihem më mirë tani.
[ndíhɛm mə mírə taní]

It's OK.

Është në rregull.
[ə́ʃtə nə réguɫ]

It's all right.

Është në rregull.
[ə́ʃtə nə réguɫ]

At the pharmacy

pharmacy (drugstore)	**farmaci** [farmatsí]
24-hour pharmacy	**farmaci 24 orë** [farmatsí ɲəzét ɛ kátər orə]
Where is the closest pharmacy?	**Ku është farmacia më e afërt?** [ku ə́ʃtə farmatsía mə ɛ áfərt?]

Is it open now?	**Është e hapur tani?** [ə́ʃtə ɛ hápur taní?]
At what time does it open?	**Në çfarë ore hapet?** [nə tʃfárə órɛ hápɛt?]
At what time does it close?	**Në çfarë ore mbyllet?** [nə tʃfárə órɛ mbýɫɛt?]

Is it far?	**Është larg?** [ə́ʃtə larg?]
Can I get there on foot?	**Mund të shkoj me këmbë deri atje?** [mund tə ʃkoj mɛ kə́mbə déri atjé?]
Can you show me on the map?	**Mund të më tregoni në hartë?** [mund tə mə trɛgóni nə hártə?]

Please give me something for ...	**Ju lutem më jepni diçka për ...** [ju lútɛm mə jépni ditʃká pər ...]
a headache	**dhimbje koke** [ðímbjɛ kókɛ]
a cough	**kollë** [kóɫə]
a cold	**ftohje** [ftóhjɛ]
the flu	**grip** [grip]

a fever	**ethe** [éθɛ]
a stomach ache	**dhimbje stomaku** [ðímbjɛ stomáku]
nausea	**të përziera** [tə pərzíɛra]
diarrhea	**diarre** [diaré]
constipation	**kapsllëk** [kapsɫə́k]
pain in the back	**dhimbje në shpinë** [ðímbjɛ nə ʃpínə]

chest pain	**dhimbje në kraharor** [ðímbjɛ nə kraharór]
side stitch	**dhimbje në brinjë** [ðímbjɛ nə bríɲə]
abdominal pain	**dhimbje barku** [ðímbjɛ bárku]

pill	**pilulë** [pilúlə]
ointment, cream	**vaj, krem** [vaj], [krɛm]
syrup	**shurup** [ʃurúp]
spray	**sprej** [sprɛj]
drops	**pika** [píka]

You need to go to the hospital.	**Duhet të shkoni në spital.** [dúhɛt tə ʃkóni nə spitál]
health insurance	**sigurim shëndetësor** [sigurím ʃəndɛtəsór]
prescription	**recetë** [rɛtsétə]
insect repellant	**mbrojtës nga insektet** [mbrójtəs ŋa insÉktɛt]
Band Aid	**leukoplast** [lɛukoplást]

The bare minimum

Excuse me, …
Më falni, …
[mə fálni, …]

Hello.
Përshëndetje.
[pərʃəndétjɛ]

Thank you.
Faleminderit.
[falɛmindérit]

Good bye.
Mirupafshim.
[mirupáfʃim]

Yes.
Po.
[po]

No.
Jo.
[jo]

I don't know.
Nuk e di.
[nuk ɛ di]

Where? | Where to? | When?
Ku? | Për ku? | Kur?
[ku? | pər ku? | kur?]

I need …
Më nevojitet …
[mə nɛvojítɛt …]

I want …
Dua …
[dúa …]

Do you have …?
Keni …?
[kéni …?]

Is there a … here?
A ka … këtu?
[a ka … kətú?]

May I …?
Mund të …?
[mund tə …?]

…, please (polite request)
…, ju lutem
[…], [ju lútɛm]

I'm looking for …
Kërkoj …
[kərkój …]

the restroom
tualet
[tualét]

an ATM
bankomat
[bankomát]

a pharmacy (drugstore)
farmaci
[farmatsí]

a hospital
spital
[spitál]

the police station
komisariat policie
[komisariát politsíɛ]

the subway
metro
[mɛtró]

a taxi	**taksi** [táksi]
the train station	**stacion treni** [statsión trɛni]

My name is ...	**Më quajnë ...** [mə cúajnə ...]
What's your name?	**Si quheni?** [si cúhɛni?]
Could you please help me?	**Ju lutem, mund të ndihmoni?** [ju lútɛm], [mund tə ndihmóni?]
I've got a problem.	**Kam një problem.** [kam ɲə problém]
I don't feel well.	**Nuk ndihem mirë.** [nuk ndíhɛm mírə]
Call an ambulance!	**Thërrisni një ambulancë!** [θərísni ɲə ambulántsə!]
May I make a call?	**Mund të bëj një telefonatë?** [mund tə bəj ɲə tɛlɛfonátə?]

I'm sorry.	**Më vjen keq.** [mə vjɛn kɛc]
You're welcome.	**Ju lutem.** [ju lútɛm]

I, me	**unë, mua** [únə], [múa]
you (inform.)	**ti** [ti]
he	**ai** [ai]
she	**ajo** [ajó]
they (masc.)	**ata** [atá]
they (fem.)	**ato** [ató]
we	**ne** [nɛ]
you (pl)	**ju** [ju]
you (sg, form.)	**ju** [ju]

ENTRANCE	**HYRJE** [hýrjɛ]
EXIT	**DALJE** [dáljɛ]
OUT OF ORDER	**NUK FUNKSIONON** [nuk funksionón]
CLOSED	**MBYLLUR** [mbýɫur]

OPEN	**HAPUR** [hápur]
FOR WOMEN	**PËR FEMRA** [pər fémra]
FOR MEN	**PËR MESHKUJ** [pər méʃkuj]

T&P BOOKS

TOPICAL VOCABULARY

This section contains more than 3,000 of the most important words.
The dictionary will provide invaluable assistance while traveling abroad, because frequently individual words are enough for you to be understood.
The dictionary includes a convenient transcription of each foreign word

T&P Books Publishing

VOCABULARY
CONTENTS

T&P Books Publishing

T&P BOOKS

BASIC CONCEPTS

T&P Books Publishing

1. Pronouns

I, me	**Unë, mua**	[unə], [múa]
you	**ti, ty**	[ti], [ty]
he	**ai**	[aí]
she	**ajo**	[ajó]
it	**ai**	[aí]
we	**ne**	[nɛ]
you (to a group)	**ju**	[ju]
they (masc.)	**ata**	[atá]
they (fem.)	**ato**	[ató]

2. Greetings. Salutations

Hello! (fam.)	**Përshëndetje!**	[pərʃəndétjɛ!]
Hello! (form.)	**Përshëndetje!**	[pərʃəndétjɛ!]
Good morning!	**Mirëmëngjes!**	[mirəmənɟés!]
Good afternoon!	**Mirëdita!**	[mirədíta!]
Good evening!	**Mirëmbrëma!**	[mirəmbrə́ma!]
to say hello	**përshëndes**	[pərʃəndés]
Hi! (hello)	**Ç'kemi!**	[tʃkémi!]
greeting (n)	**përshëndetje** (f)	[pərʃəndétjɛ]
to greet (vt)	**përshëndes**	[pərʃəndés]
How are you? (form.)	**Si jeni?**	[si jéni?]
How are you? (fam.)	**Si je?**	[si jɛ?]
What's new?	**Çfarë ka të re?**	[tʃfárə ká tə ré?]
Goodbye!	**Mirupafshim!**	[mirupáfʃim!]
Bye!	**U pafshim!**	[u páfʃim!]
See you soon!	**Shihemi së shpejti!**	[ʃíhɛmi sə ʃpéjti!]
Farewell!	**Lamtumirë!**	[lamtumírə!]
to say goodbye	**përshëndetem**	[pərʃəndétɛm]
So long!	**Tungjatjeta!**	[tunɟatjéta!]
Thank you!	**Faleminderit!**	[falɛmindérit!]
Thank you very much!	**Faleminderit shumë!**	[falɛmindérit ʃúmə!]
You're welcome	**Të lutem**	[tə lútɛm]
Don't mention it!	**Asgjë!**	[asɟé!]
It was nothing	**Asgjë**	[asɟé]
Excuse me! (fam.)	**Më fal!**	[mə fal!]

| Excuse me! (form.) | Më falni! | [mə fálni!] |
| to excuse (forgive) | fal | [fal] |

to apologize (vi)	kërkoj falje	[kərkój fáljɛ]
My apologies	Kërkoj ndjesë	[kərkój ndjésə]
I'm sorry!	Më vjen keq!	[mə vjɛn kɛc!]
to forgive (vt)	fal	[fal]
It's okay! (that's all right)	S'ka gjë!	[s'ka ɟə!]
please (adv)	të lutem	[tə lútɛm]

Don't forget!	Mos harro!	[mos haró!]
Certainly!	Sigurisht!	[siguríʃt!]
Of course not!	Sigurisht që jo!	[siguríʃt cə jo!]
Okay! (I agree)	Në rregull!	[nə réguɫ!]
That's enough!	Mjafton!	[mjaftón!]

3. Questions

Who?	Kush?	[kuʃ?]
What?	Çka?	[tʃká?]
Where? (at, in)	Ku?	[ku?]
Where (to)?	Për ku?	[pər ku?]
From where?	Nga ku?	[ŋa ku?]
When?	Kur?	[kur?]
Why? (What for?)	Pse?	[psɛ?]
Why? (~ are you crying?)	Pse?	[psɛ?]

What for?	Për çfarë arsye?	[pər tʃfárə arsýɛ?]
How? (in what way)	Si?	[si?]
What? (What kind of ...?)	Çfarë?	[tʃfárə?]
Which?	Cili?	[tsíli?]

To whom?	Kujt?	[kújt?]
About whom?	Për kë?	[pər kə?]
About what?	Për çfarë?	[pər tʃfárə?]
With whom?	Me kë?	[mɛ kə?]

| How many? How much? | Sa? | [sa?] |
| Whose? | Të kujt? | [tə kujt?] |

4. Prepositions

with (accompanied by)	me	[mɛ]
without	pa	[pa]
to (indicating direction)	për në	[pər nə]
about (talking ~ ...)	për	[pər]
before (in time)	përpara	[pərpára]
in front of ...	para ...	[pára ...]

under (beneath, below)	nën	[nən]
above (over)	mbi	[mbí]
on (atop)	mbi	[mbí]
from (off, out of)	nga	[ŋa]
of (made from)	nga	[ŋa]
in (e.g., ~ ten minutes)	për	[pər]
over (across the top of)	sipër	[sípər]

5. Function words. Adverbs. Part 1

Where? (at, in)	Ku?	[ku?]
here (adv)	këtu	[kətú]
there (adv)	atje	[atjé]
somewhere (to be)	diku	[dikú]
nowhere (not in any place)	askund	[askúnd]
by (near, beside)	afër	[áfər]
by the window	tek dritarja	[tɛk dritárja]
Where (to)?	Për ku?	[pər ku?]
here (e.g., come ~!)	këtu	[kətú]
there (e.g., to go ~)	atje	[atjé]
from here (adv)	nga këtu	[ŋa kətú]
from there (adv)	nga atje	[ŋa atjɛ]
close (adv)	pranë	[pránə]
far (adv)	larg	[larg]
near (e.g., ~ Paris)	afër	[áfər]
nearby (adv)	pranë	[pránə]
not far (adv)	jo larg	[jo lárg]
left (adj)	majtë	[májtə]
on the left	majtas	[májtas]
to the left	në të majtë	[nə tə májtə]
right (adj)	djathtë	[djáθtə]
on the right	djathtas	[djáθtas]
to the right	në të djathtë	[nə tə djáθtə]
in front (adv)	përballë	[pərbáɫə]
front (as adj)	i përparmë	[i pərpármə]
ahead (the kids ran ~)	përpara	[pərpára]
behind (adv)	prapa	[prápa]
from behind	nga prapa	[ŋa prápa]
back (towards the rear)	pas	[pas]
middle	mes (m)	[mɛs]

in the middle	në mes	[nə mɛs]
at the side	në anë	[nə anə]
everywhere (adv)	kudo	[kúdo]
around (in all directions)	përreth	[pəréθ]

from inside	nga brenda	[ŋa brénda]
somewhere (to go)	diku	[dikú]
straight (directly)	drejt	[dréjt]
back (e.g., come ~)	pas	[pas]

| from anywhere | nga kudo | [ŋa kúdo] |
| from somewhere | nga diku | [ŋa dikú] |

firstly (adv)	së pari	[sə pári]
secondly (adv)	së dyti	[sə dýti]
thirdly (adv)	së treti	[sə tréti]

suddenly (adv)	befas	[béfas]
at first (in the beginning)	në fillim	[nə fiłím]
for the first time	për herë të parë	[pər hérə tə párə]
long before …	shumë përpara …	[ʃúmə pərpára …]
anew (over again)	sërish	[səríʃ]
for good (adv)	një herë e mirë	[ɲə hérə ɛ mírə]

never (adv)	kurrë	[kúrə]
again (adv)	përsëri	[pərsərí]
now (at present)	tani	[táni]
often (adv)	shpesh	[ʃpɛʃ]
then (adv)	atëherë	[atəhérə]
urgently (quickly)	urgjent	[urɟént]
usually (adv)	zakonisht	[zakoníʃt]

by the way, …	meqë ra fjala, …	[mécə ra fjála, …]
possibly	ndoshta	[ndóʃta]
probably (adv)	mundësisht	[mundəsíʃt]
maybe (adv)	mbase	[mbásɛ]
besides …	përveç	[pərvétʃ]
that's why …	ja përse …	[ja pərsé …]
in spite of …	pavarësisht se …	[pavarəsíʃt sɛ …]
thanks to …	falë …	[fálə …]

what (pron.)	çfarë	[tʃfárə]
that (conj.)	që	[cə]
something	diçka	[ditʃká]
anything (something)	ndonji gjë	[ndoɲí ɟə]
nothing	asgjë	[asɟé]

who (pron.)	kush	[kuʃ]
someone	dikush	[dikúʃ]
somebody	dikush	[dikúʃ]
nobody	askush	[askúʃ]
nowhere (a voyage to ~)	askund	[askúnd]

| nobody's | i askujt | [i askújt] |
| somebody's | i dikujt | [i dikújt] |

so (I'm ~ glad)	aq	[ác]
also (as well)	gjithashtu	[ɟiθaʃtú]
too (as well)	gjithashtu	[ɟiθaʃtú]

6. Function words. Adverbs. Part 2

Why?	Pse?	[psɛ?]
for some reason	për një arsye	[pər ɲə arsýɛ]
because ...	sepse ...	[sɛpsé ...]
for some purpose	për ndonjë shkak	[pər ndóɲə ʃkak]

and	dhe	[ðɛ]
or	ose	[ósɛ]
but	por	[por]
for (e.g., ~ me)	për	[pər]

too (~ many people)	tepër	[tépər]
only (exclusively)	vetëm	[vétəm]
exactly (adv)	pikërisht	[pikəríʃt]
about (more or less)	rreth	[rɛθ]

approximately (adv)	përafërsisht	[pərafərsíʃt]
approximate (adj)	përafërt	[pəráfərt]
almost (adv)	pothuajse	[poθúajsɛ]
the rest	mbetje (f)	[mbétjɛ]

the other (second)	tjetri	[tjétri]
other (different)	tjetër	[tjétər]
each (adj)	çdo	[tʃdo]
any (no matter which)	çfarëdo	[tʃfarədó]
many (adj)	disa	[disá]
much (adv)	shumë	[ʃúmə]
many people	shumë njerëz	[ʃúmə ɲérəz]
all (everyone)	të gjithë	[tə ɟíθə]

in return for ...	në vend të ...	[nə vénd tə ...]
in exchange (adv)	në shkëmbim të ...	[nə ʃkəmbím tə ...]
by hand (made)	me dorë	[mɛ dórə]
hardly (negative opinion)	vështirë se ...	[vəʃtírə sɛ ...]

probably (adv)	mundësisht	[mundəsíʃt]
on purpose (intentionally)	me qëllim	[mɛ cəɫím]
by accident (adv)	aksidentalisht	[aksidɛntalíʃt]

very (adv)	shumë	[ʃúmə]
for example (adv)	për shembull	[pər ʃémbuɫ]
between	midis	[midís]

among	rreth	[rɛθ]
so much (such a lot)	kaq shumë	[kác ʃúmə]
especially (adv)	veçanërisht	[vɛtʃanəríʃt]

NUMBERS.
MISCELLANEOUS

T&P Books Publishing

0 zero	zero	[zéro]
1 one	një	[ɲə]
2 two	dy	[dy]
3 three	tre	[trɛ]
4 four	katër	[kátər]

5 five	pesë	[pésə]
6 six	gjashtë	[ɟáʃtə]
7 seven	shtatë	[ʃtátə]
8 eight	tetë	[tétə]
9 nine	nëntë	[nəntə]

10 ten	dhjetë	[ðjétə]
11 eleven	njëmbëdhjetë	[ɲəmbəðjétə]
12 twelve	dymbëdhjetë	[dymbəðjétə]
13 thirteen	trembëdhjetë	[trɛmbəðjétə]
14 fourteen	katërmbëdhjetë	[katərmbəðjétə]

15 fifteen	pesëmbëdhjetë	[pɛsəmbəðjétə]
16 sixteen	gjashtëmbëdhjetë	[ɟaʃtəmbəðjétə]
17 seventeen	shtatëmbëdhjetë	[ʃtatəmbəðjétə]
18 eighteen	tetëmbëdhjetë	[tɛtəmbəðjétə]
19 nineteen	nëntëmbëdhjetë	[nəntəmbəðjétə]

20 twenty	njëzet	[ɲəzét]
21 twenty-one	njëzet e një	[ɲəzét ɛ ɲə]
22 twenty-two	njëzet e dy	[ɲəzét ɛ dy]
23 twenty-three	njëzet e tre	[ɲəzét ɛ trɛ]

30 thirty	tridhjetë	[triðjétə]
31 thirty-one	tridhjetë e një	[triðjétə ɛ ɲə]
32 thirty-two	tridhjetë e dy	[triðjétə ɛ dy]
33 thirty-three	tridhjetë e tre	[triðjétə ɛ trɛ]

40 forty	dyzet	[dyzét]
41 forty-one	dyzet e një	[dyzét ɛ ɲə]
42 forty-two	dyzet e dy	[dyzét ɛ dy]
43 forty-three	dyzet e tre	[dyzét ɛ trɛ]

50 fifty	pesëdhjetë	[pɛsəðjétə]
51 fifty-one	pesëdhjetë e një	[pɛsəðjétə ɛ ɲə]
52 fifty-two	pesëdhjetë e dy	[pɛsəðjétə ɛ dy]
53 fifty-three	pesëdhjetë e tre	[pɛsəðjétə ɛ trɛ]
60 sixty	gjashtëdhjetë	[ɟaʃtəðjétə]

61 sixty-one	gjashtëdhjetë e një	[ʝaʃtəðjétə ɛ ɲə]
62 sixty-two	gjashtëdhjetë e dy	[ʝaʃtəðjétə ɛ dý]
63 sixty-three	gjashtëdhjetë e tre	[ʝaʃtəðjétə ɛ tré]

70 seventy	shtatëdhjetë	[ʃtatəðjétə]
71 seventy-one	shtatëdhjetë e një	[ʃtatəðjétə ɛ ɲə]
72 seventy-two	shtatëdhjetë e dy	[ʃtatəðjétə ɛ dy]
73 seventy-three	shtatëdhjetë e tre	[ʃtatəðjétə ɛ trɛ]

80 eighty	tetëdhjetë	[tɛtəðjétə]
81 eighty-one	tetëdhjetë e një	[tɛtəðjétə ɛ ɲə]
82 eighty-two	tetëdhjetë e dy	[tɛtəðjétə ɛ dy]
83 eighty-three	tetëdhjetë e tre	[tɛtəðjétə ɛ trɛ]

90 ninety	nëntëdhjetë	[nəntəðjétə]
91 ninety-one	nëntëdhjetë e një	[nəntəðjétə ɛ ɲə]
92 ninety-two	nëntëdhjetë e dy	[nəntəðjétə ɛ dy]
93 ninety-three	nëntëdhjetë e tre	[nəntəðjétə ɛ trɛ]

8. Cardinal numbers. Part 2

100 one hundred	njëqind	[nəcínd]
200 two hundred	dyqind	[dycínd]
300 three hundred	treqind	[trɛcínd]
400 four hundred	katërqind	[katərcínd]
500 five hundred	pesëqind	[pɛsəcínd]

600 six hundred	gjashtëqind	[ʝaʃtəcínd]
700 seven hundred	shtatëqind	[ʃtatəcínd]
800 eight hundred	tetëqind	[tɛtəcínd]
900 nine hundred	nëntëqind	[nəntəcínd]

1000 one thousand	një mijë	[ɲə míjə]
2000 two thousand	dy mijë	[dy míjə]
3000 three thousand	tre mijë	[trɛ míjə]
10000 ten thousand	dhjetë mijë	[ðjétə míjə]
one hundred thousand	njëqind mijë	[ɲəcínd míjə]
million	milion (m)	[milión]
billion	miliardë (f)	[miliárdə]

9. Ordinal numbers

first (adj)	i pari	[i pári]
second (adj)	i dyti	[i dýti]
third (adj)	i treti	[i tréti]
fourth (adj)	i katërti	[i kátərti]
fifth (adj)	i pesti	[i pésti]
sixth (adj)	i gjashti	[i ʝáʃti]

seventh (adj)	**i shtati**	[i ʃtáti]
eighth (adj)	**i teti**	[i téti]
ninth (adj)	**i nënti**	[i nə́nti]
tenth (adj)	**i dhjeti**	[i ðjéti]

TᴇP BOOKS

COLOURS. UNITS OF MEASUREMENT

T&P Books Publishing

10. Colors

color	ngjyrë (f)	[ɲɟýrə]
shade (tint)	nuancë (f)	[nuántsə]
hue	tonalitet (m)	[tonalitét]
rainbow	ylber (m)	[ylbér]

white (adj)	e bardhë	[ɛ bárðə]
black (adj)	e zezë	[ɛ zézə]
gray (adj)	gri	[gri]

green (adj)	jeshile	[jɛʃílɛ]
yellow (adj)	e verdhë	[ɛ vérðə]
red (adj)	e kuqe	[ɛ kúcɛ]
blue (adj)	blu	[blu]
light blue (adj)	bojëqielli	[bojəciéti]
pink (adj)	rozë	[rózə]
orange (adj)	portokalli	[portokáti]
violet (adj)	bojëvjollcë	[bojəvjóttsə]
brown (adj)	kafe	[káfɛ]

golden (adj)	e artë	[ɛ ártə]
silvery (adj)	e argjendtë	[ɛ arɟéndtə]
beige (adj)	bezhë	[béʒə]
cream (adj)	krem	[krɛm]
turquoise (adj)	e bruztë	[ɛ brúztə]
cherry red (adj)	qershi	[cɛrʃí]
lilac (adj)	jargavan	[jargaván]
crimson (adj)	e kuqe e thellë	[ɛ kúcɛ ɛ θétə]

light (adj)	e hapur	[ɛ hápur]
dark (adj)	e errët	[ɛ érət]
bright, vivid (adj)	e ndritshme	[ɛ ndrítʃmɛ]

colored (pencils)	e ngjyrosur	[ɛ nɟyrósur]
color (e.g., ~ film)	ngjyrë	[nɟýrə]
black-and-white (adj)	bardhë e zi	[bárðə ɛ zi]
plain (one-colored)	njëngjyrëshe	[nənɟýrəʃɛ]
multicolored (adj)	shumëngjyrëshe	[ʃumənɟýrəʃɛ]

11. Units of measurement

| weight | peshë (f) | [péʃə] |
| length | gjatësi (f) | [ɟatəsí] |

width	gjerësi (f)	[ɟɛrəsí]
height	lartësi (f)	[lartəsí]
depth	thellësi (f)	[θɛłəsí]
volume	vëllim (m)	[vətím]
area	sipërfaqe (f)	[sipərfácɛ]

gram	gram (m)	[gram]
milligram	miligram (m)	[miligrám]
kilogram	kilogram (m)	[kilográm]
ton	ton (m)	[ton]
pound	paund (m)	[páund]
ounce	ons (m)	[ons]

meter	metër (m)	[métər]
millimeter	milimetër (m)	[milimétər]
centimeter	centimetër (m)	[tsɛntimétər]
kilometer	kilometër (m)	[kilométər]
mile	milje (f)	[míljɛ]

inch	inç (m)	[intʃ]
foot	këmbë (f)	[kémbə]
yard	jard (m)	[járd]

square meter	metër katror (m)	[métər katrór]
hectare	hektar (m)	[hɛktár]
liter	litër (m)	[lítər]
degree	gradë (f)	[grádə]
volt	volt (m)	[volt]
ampere	amper (m)	[ampér]
horsepower	kuaj-fuqi (f)	[kúaj-fucí]

quantity	sasi (f)	[sasí]
a little bit of …	pak …	[pak …]
half	gjysmë (f)	[ɟýsmə]
dozen	dyzinë (f)	[dyzínə]
piece (item)	copë (f)	[tsópə]

| size | madhësi (f) | [maðəsí] |
| scale (map ~) | shkallë (f) | [ʃkáłə] |

minimal (adj)	minimale	[minimálɛ]
the smallest (adj)	më i vogli	[mə i vógli]
medium (adj)	i mesëm	[i mésəm]
maximal (adj)	maksimale	[maksimálɛ]
the largest (adj)	më i madhi	[mə i máði]

12. Containers

| canning jar (glass ~) | kavanoz (m) | [kavanóz] |
| can | kanoçe (f) | [kanótʃɛ] |

bucket	**kovë** (f)	[kóvə]
barrel	**fuçi** (f)	[futʃí]
wash basin (e.g., plastic ~)	**legen** (m)	[lɛgén]
tank (100L water ~)	**tank** (m)	[tank]
hip flask	**faqore** (f)	[facórɛ]
jerrycan	**bidon** (m)	[bidón]
tank (e.g., tank car)	**cisternë** (f)	[tsistérnə]
mug	**tas** (m)	[tas]
cup (of coffee, etc.)	**filxhan** (m)	[fildʒán]
saucer	**pjatë filxhani** (f)	[pjátə fildʒáni]
glass (tumbler)	**gotë** (f)	[gótə]
wine glass	**gotë vere** (f)	[gótə vérɛ]
stock pot (soup pot)	**tenxhere** (f)	[tɛndʒérɛ]
bottle (~ of wine)	**shishe** (f)	[ʃíʃɛ]
neck (of the bottle, etc.)	**grykë**	[grýkə]
carafe (decanter)	**brokë** (f)	[brókə]
pitcher	**shtambë** (f)	[ʃtámbə]
vessel (container)	**enë** (f)	[énə]
pot (crock, stoneware ~)	**enë** (f)	[énə]
vase	**vazo** (f)	[vázo]
flacon, bottle (perfume ~)	**shishe** (f)	[ʃíʃɛ]
vial, small bottle	**shishkë** (f)	[ʃíʃkə]
tube (of toothpaste)	**tubet** (f)	[tubét]
sack (bag)	**thes** (m)	[θɛs]
bag (paper ~, plastic ~)	**qese** (f)	[césɛ]
pack (of cigarettes, etc.)	**paketë** (f)	[pakétə]
box (e.g., shoebox)	**kuti** (f)	[kutí]
crate	**arkë** (f)	[árkə]
basket	**shportë** (f)	[ʃpórtə]

T&P BOOKS

MAIN VERBS

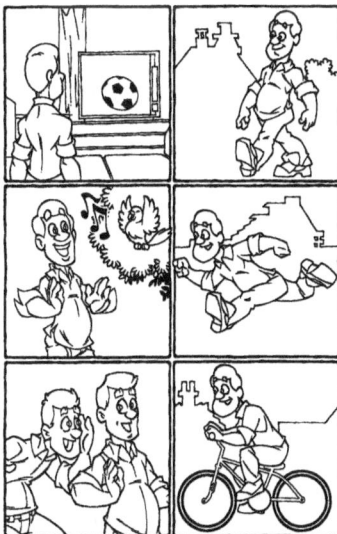

T&P Books Publishing

13. The most important verbs. Part 1

to advise (vt)	**këshilloj**	[kəʃiɫój]
to agree (say yes)	**bie dakord**	[bíɛ dakórd]
to answer (vi, vt)	**përgjigjem**	[pərɟíɟɛm]
to apologize (vi)	**kërkoj falje**	[kərkój fáljɛ]
to arrive (vi)	**arrij**	[aríj]
to ask (~ oneself)	**pyes**	[pýɛs]
to ask (~ sb to do sth)	**pyes**	[pýɛs]
to be (vi)	**jam**	[jam]
to be afraid	**kam frikë**	[kam fríkə]
to be hungry	**kam uri**	[kam urí]
to be interested in …	**interesohem …**	[intɛrɛsóhɛm …]
to be needed	**nevojitet**	[nɛvojítɛt]
to be surprised	**çuditem**	[tʃudítɛm]
to be thirsty	**kam etje**	[kam étjɛ]
to begin (vt)	**filloj**	[fiɫój]
to belong to …	**përkas …**	[pərkás …]
to boast (vi)	**mburrem**	[mbúrɛm]
to break (split into pieces)	**ndahem**	[ndáhɛm]
to call (~ for help)	**thërras**	[θərás]
can (v aux)	**mund**	[mund]
to catch (vt)	**kap**	[kap]
to change (vt)	**ndryshoj**	[ndryʃój]
to choose (select)	**zgjedh**	[zɟɛð]
to come down (the stairs)	**zbres**	[zbrɛs]
to compare (vt)	**krahasoj**	[krahasój]
to complain (vi, vt)	**ankohem**	[ankóhɛm]
to confuse (mix up)	**ngatërroj**	[ŋatərój]
to continue (vt)	**vazhdoj**	[vaʒdój]
to control (vt)	**kontrolloj**	[kontroɫój]
to cook (dinner)	**gatuaj**	[gatúaj]
to cost (vt)	**kushton**	[kuʃtón]
to count (add up)	**numëroj**	[numərój]
to count on …	**mbështetem …**	[mbəʃtétɛm …]
to create (vt)	**krijoj**	[krijój]
to cry (weep)	**qaj**	[caj]

14. The most important verbs. Part 2

to deceive (vi, vt)	mashtroj	[maʃtrój]
to decorate (tree, street)	zbukuroj	[zbukurój]
to defend (a country, etc.)	mbroj	[mbrój]
to demand (request firmly)	kërkoj	[kərkój]
to dig (vt)	gërmoj	[gərmój]

to discuss (vt)	diskutoj	[diskutój]
to do (vt)	bëj	[bəj]
to doubt (have doubts)	dyshoj	[dyʃój]
to drop (let fall)	lëshoj	[ləʃój]
to enter (room, house, etc.)	hyj	[hyj]

to excuse (forgive)	fal	[fal]
to exist (vi)	ekzistoj	[ɛkzistój]
to expect (foresee)	parashikoj	[paraʃikój]

to explain (vt)	shpjegoj	[ʃpjɛgój]
to fall (vi)	bie	[bíɛ]

to find (vt)	gjej	[ɟéj]
to finish (vt)	përfundoj	[pərfundój]
to fly (vi)	fluturoj	[fluturój]

to follow ... (come after)	ndjek ...	[ndjék ...]
to forget (vi, vt)	harroj	[harój]

to forgive (vt)	fal	[fal]
to give (vt)	jap	[jap]

to give a hint	aludoj	[aludój]
to go (on foot)	ec në këmbë	[ɛts nə kémbə]

to go for a swim	notoj	[notój]
to go out (for dinner, etc.)	dal	[dal]
to guess (the answer)	hamendësoj	[hamɛndəsój]

to have (vt)	kam	[kam]
to have breakfast	ha mëngjes	[ha mənɟés]
to have dinner	ha darkë	[ha dárkə]

to have lunch	ha drekë	[ha drékə]
to hear (vt)	dëgjoj	[dəɟój]

to help (vt)	ndihmoj	[ndihmój]
to hide (vt)	fsheh	[fʃéh]
to hope (vi, vt)	shpresoj	[ʃprɛsój]
to hunt (vi, vt)	dal për gjah	[dál pər ɟáh]
to hurry (vi)	nxitoj	[ndzitój]

15. The most important verbs. Part 3

to inform (vt)	informoj	[informój]
to insist (vi, vt)	këmbëngul	[kəmbəɲúl]
to insult (vt)	fyej	[fýɛj]
to invite (vt)	ftoj	[ftoj]
to joke (vi)	bëj shaka	[bəj ʃaká]
to keep (vt)	mbaj	[mbáj]
to keep silent, to hush	hesht	[hɛʃt]
to kill (vt)	vras	[vras]
to know (sb)	njoh	[ɲóh]
to know (sth)	di	[di]
to laugh (vi)	qesh	[cɛʃ]
to liberate (city, etc.)	çliroj	[tʃlirój]
to like (I like ...)	pëlqej	[pəlcéj]
to look for ... (search)	kërkoj ...	[kərkój ...]
to love (sb)	dashuroj	[daʃurój]
to make a mistake	gaboj	[gabój]
to manage, to run	drejtoj	[drɛjtój]
to mean (signify)	nënkuptoj	[nənkuptój]
to mention (talk about)	përmend	[pərménd]
to miss (school, etc.)	humbas	[humbás]
to notice (see)	vërej	[vəréj]
to object (vi, vt)	kundërshtoj	[kundərʃtój]
to observe (see)	vëzhgoj	[vəʒgój]
to open (vt)	hap	[hap]
to order (meal, etc.)	porosis	[porosís]
to order (mil.)	urdhëroj	[urðərój]
to own (possess)	zotëroj	[zotərój]
to participate (vi)	marr pjesë	[mar pjésə]
to pay (vi, vt)	paguaj	[pagúaj]
to permit (vt)	lejoj	[lɛjój]
to plan (vt)	planifikoj	[planifikój]
to play (children)	luaj	[lúaj]
to pray (vi, vt)	lutem	[lútɛm]
to prefer (vt)	preferoj	[prɛfɛrój]
to promise (vt)	premtoj	[prɛmtój]
to pronounce (vt)	shqiptoj	[ʃciptój]
to propose (vt)	propozoj	[propozój]
to punish (vt)	ndëshkoj	[ndəʃkój]

16. The most important verbs. Part 4

to read (vi, vt)	lexoj	[lɛdzój]
to recommend (vt)	rekomandoj	[rɛkomandój]

to refuse (vi, vt)	refuzoj	[rɛfuzój]
to regret (be sorry)	pendohem	[pɛndóhɛm]
to rent (sth from sb)	marr me qira	[mar mɛ cirá]

to repeat (say again)	përsëris	[pərsərís]
to reserve, to book	rezervoj	[rɛzɛrvój]
to run (vi)	vrapoj	[vrapój]
to save (rescue)	shpëtoj	[ʃpətój]
to say (~ thank you)	them	[θɛm]

to scold (vt)	qortoj	[cortój]
to see (vt)	shikoj	[ʃikój]
to sell (vt)	shes	[ʃɛs]
to send (vt)	dërgoj	[dərgój]
to shoot (vi)	qëlloj	[cətój]

to shout (vi)	bërtas	[bərtás]
to show (vt)	tregoj	[trɛgój]
to sign (document)	nënshkruaj	[nənʃkrúaj]
to sit down (vi)	ulem	[úlɛm]

to smile (vi)	buzëqesh	[buzəcéʃ]
to speak (vi, vt)	flas	[flas]
to steal (money, etc.)	vjedh	[vjɛð]
to stop (for pause, etc.)	ndaloj	[ndalój]
to stop (please ~ calling me)	ndaloj	[ndalój]

to study (vt)	studioj	[studiój]
to swim (vi)	notoj	[notój]
to take (vt)	marr	[mar]
to think (vi, vt)	mendoj	[mɛndój]
to threaten (vt)	kërcënoj	[kərtsənój]

to touch (with hands)	prek	[prɛk]
to translate (vt)	përkthej	[pərkθéj]
to trust (vt)	besoj	[bɛsój]
to try (attempt)	përpiqem	[pərpícɛm]
to turn (e.g., ~ left)	kthej	[kθɛj]

to underestimate (vt)	nënvlerësoj	[nənvlɛrəsój]
to understand (vt)	kuptoj	[kuptój]
to unite (vt)	bashkoj	[baʃkój]
to wait (vt)	pres	[prɛs]

to want (wish, desire)	dëshiroj	[dəʃirój]
to warn (vt)	paralajmëroj	[paralajmərój]
to work (vi)	punoj	[punój]
to write (vt)	shkruaj	[ʃkrúaj]
to write down	mbaj shënim	[mbáj ʃəním]

TIME. CALENDAR

T&P Books Publishing

17. Weekdays

Monday	**E hënë** (f)	[ɛ hénə]
Tuesday	**E martë** (f)	[ɛ mártə]
Wednesday	**E mërkurë** (f)	[ɛ mərkúrə]
Thursday	**E enjte** (f)	[ɛ éɲtɛ]
Friday	**E premte** (f)	[ɛ prémtɛ]
Saturday	**E shtunë** (f)	[ɛ ʃtúnə]
Sunday	**E dielë** (f)	[ɛ díɛlə]
today (adv)	**sot**	[sot]
tomorrow (adv)	**nesër**	[nésər]
the day after tomorrow	**pasnesër**	[pasnésər]
yesterday (adv)	**dje**	[djé]
the day before yesterday	**pardje**	[pardjé]
day	**ditë** (f)	[dítə]
working day	**ditë pune** (f)	[dítə púnɛ]
public holiday	**festë kombëtare** (f)	[féstə kombətárɛ]
day off	**ditë pushim** (m)	[dítə puʃím]
weekend	**fundjavë** (f)	[fundjávə]
all day long	**gjithë ditën**	[ɟíθə dítən]
the next day (adv)	**ditën pasardhëse**	[dítən pasárðəsɛ]
two days ago	**dy ditë më parë**	[dy dítə mə párə]
the day before	**një ditë më parë**	[ɲə dítə mə párə]
daily (adj)	**ditor**	[ditór]
every day (adv)	**çdo ditë**	[tʃdo dítə]
week	**javë** (f)	[jávə]
last week (adv)	**javën e kaluar**	[jávən ɛ kalúar]
next week (adv)	**javën e ardhshme**	[jávən ɛ árðʃmɛ]
weekly (adj)	**javor**	[javór]
every week (adv)	**çdo javë**	[tʃdo jávə]
twice a week	**dy herë në javë**	[dy hérə nə jávə]
every Tuesday	**çdo të martë**	[tʃdo tə mártə]

18. Hours. Day and night

morning	**mëngjes** (m)	[məɲɟés]
in the morning	**në mëngjes**	[nə məɲɟés]
noon, midday	**mesditë** (f)	[mɛsdítə]
in the afternoon	**pasdite**	[pasdítɛ]
evening	**mbrëmje** (f)	[mbrémjɛ]

in the evening	në mbrëmje	[nə mbrə́mjɛ]
night	natë (f)	[nátə]
at night	natën	[nátən]
midnight	mesnatë (f)	[mɛsnátə]

second	sekondë (f)	[sɛkóndə]
minute	minutë (f)	[minútə]
hour	orë (f)	[órə]
half an hour	gjysmë ore (f)	[ɟýsmə órɛ]
a quarter-hour	çerek ore (m)	[tʃɛrék órɛ]
fifteen minutes	pesëmbëdhjetë minuta	[pɛsəmbəðjétə minúta]
24 hours	24 orë	[nəzét ɛ kátər órə]

sunrise	agim (m)	[agím]
dawn	agim (m)	[agím]
early morning	mëngjes herët (m)	[mənɟés hérət]
sunset	perëndim dielli (m)	[pɛrəndím diéɬi]

early in the morning	herët në mëngjes	[hérət nə mənɟés]
this morning	sot në mëngjes	[sot nə mənɟés]
tomorrow morning	nesër në mëngjes	[nésər nə mənɟés]

this afternoon	sot pasdite	[sot pasdítɛ]
in the afternoon	pasdite	[pasdítɛ]
tomorrow afternoon	nesër pasdite	[nésər pasdítɛ]

| tonight (this evening) | sonte në mbrëmje | [sóntɛ nə mbrəmjɛ] |
| tomorrow night | nesër në mbrëmje | [nésər nə mbrə́mjɛ] |

at 3 o'clock sharp	në orën 3 fiks	[nə órən trɛ fiks]
about 4 o'clock	rreth orës 4	[rɛθ órəs kátər]
by 12 o'clock	deri në orën 12	[déri nə órən dymbəðjétə]

in 20 minutes	për 20 minuta	[pər ɲəzét minúta]
in an hour	për një orë	[pər ɲə órə]
on time (adv)	në orar	[nə orár]

a quarter to ...	çerek ...	[tʃɛrék ...]
within an hour	brenda një ore	[brénda ɲə órɛ]
every 15 minutes	çdo 15 minuta	[tʃdo pɛsəmbəðjétə minúta]
round the clock	gjithë ditën	[ɟíθə dítən]

19. Months. Seasons

January	Janar (m)	[janár]
February	Shkurt (m)	[ʃkurt]
March	Mars (m)	[mars]
April	Prill (m)	[priɬ]
May	Maj (m)	[maj]
June	Qershor (m)	[cɛrʃór]

July	**Korrik** (m)	[korík]
August	**Gusht** (m)	[guʃt]
September	**Shtator** (m)	[ʃtatór]
October	**Tetor** (m)	[tɛtór]
November	**Nëntor** (m)	[nəntór]
December	**Dhjetor** (m)	[ðjɛtór]

spring	**pranverë** (f)	[pranvérə]
in spring	**në pranverë**	[nə pranvérə]
spring (as adj)	**pranveror**	[pranvɛrór]

summer	**verë** (f)	[vérə]
in summer	**në verë**	[nə vérə]
summer (as adj)	**veror**	[vɛrór]

fall	**vjeshtë** (f)	[vjéʃtə]
in fall	**në vjeshtë**	[nə vjéʃtə]
fall (as adj)	**vjeshtor**	[vjéʃtor]

winter	**dimër** (m)	[dímər]
in winter	**në dimër**	[nə dímər]
winter (as adj)	**dimëror**	[dimərór]

month	**muaj** (m)	[múaj]
this month	**këtë muaj**	[kətə múaj]
next month	**muajin tjetër**	[múajin tjétər]
last month	**muajin e kaluar**	[múajin ɛ kalúar]

a month ago	**para një muaji**	[pára ɲə múaji]
in a month (a month later)	**pas një muaji**	[pas ɲə múaji]
in 2 months (2 months later)	**pas dy muajsh**	[pas dy múajʃ]
the whole month	**gjithë muajin**	[ɟíθə múajin]
all month long	**gjatë gjithë muajit**	[ɟátə ɟíθə múajit]

monthly (~ magazine)	**mujor**	[mujór]
monthly (adv)	**mujor**	[mujór]
every month	**çdo muaj**	[tʃdo múaj]
twice a month	**dy herë në muaj**	[dy hérə nə múaj]

year	**vit** (m)	[vit]
this year	**këtë vit**	[kətə vít]
next year	**vitin tjetër**	[vítin tjétər]
last year	**vitin e kaluar**	[vítin ɛ kalúar]

a year ago	**para një viti**	[pára ɲə víti]
in a year	**për një vit**	[pər ɲə vit]
in two years	**për dy vite**	[pər dy vítɛ]
the whole year	**gjithë vitin**	[ɟíθə vítin]
all year long	**gjatë gjithë vitit**	[ɟátə ɟíθə vítit]
every year	**çdo vit**	[tʃdo vít]
annual (adj)	**vjetor**	[vjɛtór]

annually (adv)	çdo vit	[tʃdo vít]
4 times a year	4 herë në vit	[kátər hérə nə vit]
date (e.g., today's ~)	datë (f)	[dátə]
date (e.g., ~ of birth)	data (f)	[dáta]
calendar	kalendar (m)	[kalɛndár]
half a year	gjysmë viti	[ɟýsmə víti]
six months	gjashtë muaj	[ɟáʃtə múaj]
season (summer, etc.)	stinë (f)	[stínə]
century	shekull (m)	[ʃékuɫ]

TRAVEL. HOTEL

USD CAD
EUR CHF
JPY HKD
GBP CNY

RECEPTION

T&P Books Publishing

20. Trip. Travel

tourism, travel	**turizëm** (m)	[turízəm]
tourist	**turist** (m)	[turíst]
trip, voyage	**udhëtim** (m)	[uðətím]
adventure	**aventurë** (f)	[avɛntúrə]
trip, journey	**udhëtim** (m)	[uðətím]
vacation	**pushim** (m)	[puʃím]
to be on vacation	**jam me pushime**	[jam mɛ puʃímɛ]
rest	**pushim** (m)	[puʃím]
train	**tren** (m)	[trɛn]
by train	**me tren**	[mɛ trén]
airplane	**avion** (m)	[avión]
by airplane	**me avion**	[mɛ avión]
by car	**me makinë**	[mɛ makínə]
by ship	**me anije**	[mɛ aníjɛ]
luggage	**bagazh** (m)	[bagáʒ]
suitcase	**valixhe** (f)	[valídʒɛ]
luggage cart	**karrocë bagazhesh** (f)	[karótsə bagáʒɛʃ]
passport	**pasaportë** (f)	[pasapórtə]
visa	**vizë** (f)	[vízə]
ticket	**biletë** (f)	[bilétə]
air ticket	**biletë avioni** (f)	[bilétə avióni]
guidebook	**guidë turistike** (f)	[guídə turistíkɛ]
map (tourist ~)	**hartë** (f)	[hártə]
area (rural ~)	**zonë** (f)	[zónə]
place, site	**vend** (m)	[vɛnd]
exotica (n)	**ekzotikë** (f)	[ɛkzotíkə]
exotic (adj)	**ekzotik**	[ɛkzotík]
amazing (adj)	**mahnitëse**	[mahnítəsɛ]
group	**grup** (m)	[grup]
excursion, sightseeing tour	**ekskursion** (m)	[ɛkskursión]
guide (person)	**udhërrëfyes** (m)	[uðərəfýɛs]

21. Hotel

hotel, inn	**hotel** (m)	[hotél]
motel	**motel** (m)	[motél]

three-star (~ hotel)	me tre yje	[mɛ trɛ ýjɛ]
five-star	me pesë yje	[mɛ pésə ýjɛ]
to stay (in a hotel, etc.)	qëndroj	[cəndrój]

room	dhomë (f)	[ðómə]
single room	dhomë teke (f)	[ðómə tékɛ]
double room	dhomë dyshe (f)	[ðómə dýʃɛ]
to book a room	rezervoj një dhomë	[rɛzɛrvój ɲə ðómə]

half board	gjysmë-pension (m)	[ɟýsmə-pɛnsión]
full board	pension i plotë (m)	[pɛnsión i plótə]

with bath	me banjo	[mɛ báɲo]
with shower	me dush	[mɛ dúʃ]
satellite television	televizor satelitor (m)	[tɛlɛvizór satɛlitór]
air-conditioner	kondicioner (m)	[konditsionér]
towel	peshqir (m)	[pɛʃcír]
key	çelës (m)	[tʃéləs]

administrator	administrator (m)	[administratór]
chambermaid	pastruese (f)	[pastrúɛsɛ]
porter, bellboy	portier (m)	[portiér]
doorman	portier (m)	[portiér]

restaurant	restorant (m)	[rɛstoránt]
pub, bar	pab (m), pijetore (f)	[pab], [pijɛtórɛ]
breakfast	mëngjes (m)	[mənɟés]
dinner	darkë (f)	[dárkə]
buffet	bufe (f)	[bufé]

lobby	holl (m)	[hoɫ]
elevator	ashensor (m)	[aʃɛnsór]

DO NOT DISTURB	MOS SHQETËSONI	[mos ʃcɛtəsóni]
NO SMOKING	NDALOHET DUHANI	[ndalóhɛt duháni]

22. Sightseeing

monument	monument (m)	[monumént]
fortress	kala (f)	[kalá]
palace	pallat (m)	[paɫát]
castle	kështjellë (f)	[kəʃtjéɫə]
tower	kullë (f)	[kúɫə]
mausoleum	mauzoleum (m)	[mauzolɛúm]

architecture	arkitekturë (f)	[arkitɛktúrə]
medieval (adj)	mesjetare	[mɛsjɛtárɛ]
ancient (adj)	e lashtë	[ɛ láʃtə]
national (adj)	kombëtare	[kombətárɛ]
famous (monument, etc.)	i famshëm	[i fámʃəm]

tourist	**turist** (m)	[turíst]
guide (person)	**udhërrëfyes** (m)	[uðərəfýɛs]
excursion, sightseeing tour	**ekskursion** (m)	[ɛkskursión]
to show (vt)	**tregoj**	[trɛgój]
to tell (vt)	**dëftoj**	[dəftój]
to find (vt)	**gjej**	[ɟéj]
to get lost (lose one's way)	**humbas**	[humbás]
map (e.g., subway ~)	**hartë** (f)	[hártə]
map (e.g., city ~)	**hartë** (f)	[hártə]
souvenir, gift	**suvenir** (m)	[suvɛnír]
gift shop	**dyqan dhuratash** (m)	[dycán ðurátaʃ]
to take pictures	**bëj foto**	[bəj fóto]
to have one's picture taken	**bëj fotografi**	[bəj fotografí]

T&P BOOKS

TRANSPORTATION

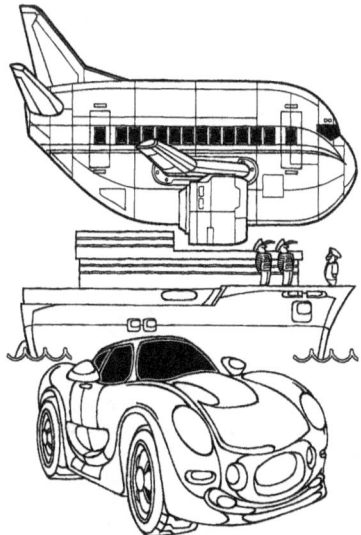

T&P Books Publishing

airport	aeroport (m)	[aɛropórt]
airplane	avion (m)	[avión]
airline	kompani ajrore (f)	[kompaní ajrórɛ]
air traffic controller	kontroll i trafikut ajror (m)	[kontrółl i trafíkut ajrór]

departure	nisje (f)	[nísjɛ]
arrival	arritje (f)	[arítjɛ]
to arrive (by plane)	arrij me avion	[aríj mɛ avión]

| departure time | nisja (f) | [nísja] |
| arrival time | arritja (f) | [arítja] |

| to be delayed | vonesë | [vonésə] |
| flight delay | vonesë avioni (f) | [vonésə avióni] |

information board	ekrani i informacioneve (m)	[ɛkráni i informatsiónɛvɛ]
information	informacion (m)	[informatsión]
to announce (vt)	njoftoj	[ɲoftój]
flight (e.g., next ~)	fluturim (m)	[fluturím]

| customs | doganë (f) | [dogánə] |
| customs officer | doganier (m) | [doganiér] |

customs declaration	deklarim doganor (m)	[dɛklarím doganór]
to fill out (vt)	plotësoj	[plotəsój]
to fill out the declaration	plotësoj deklaratën	[plotəsój dɛklarátən]
passport control	kontroll pasaportash (m)	[kontrółl pasapórtaʃ]

luggage	bagazh (m)	[bagáʒ]
hand luggage	bagazh dore (m)	[bagáʒ dórɛ]
luggage cart	karrocë bagazhesh (f)	[karótsə bagáʒɛʃ]

landing	aterrim (m)	[atɛrím]
landing strip	pistë aterrimi (f)	[pístə atɛrími]
to land (vi)	aterroj	[atɛrój]
airstair (passenger stair)	shkallë avioni (f)	[ʃkáłə avióni]

check-in	regjistrim (m)	[rɛɉistrím]
check-in counter	sportel regjistrimi (m)	[sportél rɛɉistrími]
to check-in (vi)	regjistrohem	[rɛɉistróhɛm]
boarding pass	biletë e hyrjes (f)	[bilétə ɛ hýrjɛs]
departure gate	porta e nisjes (f)	[pórta ɛ nísjɛs]
transit	transit (m)	[transít]

to wait (vt)	pres	[prɛs]
departure lounge	salla e nisjes (f)	[sáɫa ɛ nísjɛs]
to see off	përcjell	[pərtsjéɫ]
to say goodbye	përshëndetem	[pərʃəndétɛm]

24. Airplane

airplane	avion (m)	[avión]
air ticket	biletë avioni (f)	[bilétə avióni]
airline	kompani ajrore (f)	[kompaní ajrórɛ]
airport	aeroport (m)	[aɛropórt]
supersonic (adj)	supersonik	[supɛrsoník]

captain	kapiten (m)	[kapitén]
crew	ekip (m)	[ɛkíp]
pilot	pilot (m)	[pilót]
flight attendant (fem.)	stjuardesë (f)	[stjuardésə]
navigator	navigues (m)	[navigúɛs]

wings	krahë (pl)	[kráhə]
tail	bisht (m)	[biʃt]
cockpit	kabinë (f)	[kabínə]
engine	motor (m)	[motór]
undercarriage (landing gear)	karrel (m)	[karél]
turbine	turbinë (f)	[turbínə]

propeller	helikë (f)	[hɛlíkə]
black box	kuti e zezë (f)	[kutí ɛ zézə]
yoke (control column)	timon (m)	[timón]
fuel	karburant (m)	[karburánt]

safety card	udhëzime sigurie (pl)	[uðəzímɛ siguríɛ]
oxygen mask	maskë oksigjeni (f)	[máskə oksiɟéni]
uniform	uniformë (f)	[unifórmə]
life vest	jelek shpëtimi (m)	[jɛlék ʃpətími]
parachute	parashutë (f)	[paraʃútə]

takeoff	ngritje (f)	[ŋrítjɛ]
to take off (vi)	fluturon	[fluturón]
runway	pista e fluturimit (f)	[písta ɛ fluturímit]

visibility	shikueshmëri (f)	[ʃikuɛʃmərí]
flight (act of flying)	fluturim (m)	[fluturím]
altitude	lartësi (f)	[lartəsí]
air pocket	xhep ajri (m)	[dʒɛp ájri]

seat	karrige (f)	[karígɛ]
headphones	kufje (f)	[kúfjɛ]
folding tray (tray table)	tabaka (f)	[tabaká]

| airplane window | dritare avioni (f) | [dritárɛ avióni] |
| aisle | korridor (m) | [koridór] |

25. Train

train	tren (m)	[trɛn]
commuter train	tren elektrik (m)	[trɛn ɛlɛktrík]
express train	tren ekspres (m)	[trɛn ɛksprés]
diesel locomotive	lokomotivë me naftë (f)	[lokomótivə mɛ náftə]
steam locomotive	lokomotivë me avull (f)	[lokomótivə mɛ ávuł]

| passenger car | vagon (m) | [vagón] |
| dining car | vagon restorant (m) | [vagón rɛstoránt] |

rails	shina (pl)	[ʃína]
railroad	hekurudhë (f)	[hɛkurúðə]
railway tie	traversë (f)	[travérsə]

platform (railway ~)	platformë (f)	[platfórmə]
track (~ 1, 2, etc.)	binar (m)	[binár]
semaphore	semafor (m)	[sɛmafór]
station	stacion (m)	[statsión]

engineer (train driver)	makinist (m)	[makiníst]
porter (of luggage)	portier (m)	[portiér]
car attendant	konduktor (m)	[konduktór]
passenger	pasagjer (m)	[pasaɟér]
conductor (ticket inspector)	konduktor (m)	[konduktór]

| corridor (in train) | korridor (m) | [koridór] |
| emergency brake | frena urgjence (f) | [fréna urɟéntsɛ] |

compartment	ndarje (f)	[ndárjɛ]
berth	kat (m)	[kat]
upper berth	kati i sipërm (m)	[káti i sípərm]
lower berth	kati i poshtëm (m)	[káti i póʃtəm]
bed linen, bedding	shtroje shtrati (pl)	[ʃtrójə ʃtráti]

ticket	biletë (f)	[bilétə]
schedule	orar (m)	[orár]
information display	tabelë e informatave (f)	[tabélə ɛ informátavɛ]

to leave, to depart	niset	[nísɛt]
departure (of train)	nisje (f)	[nísjɛ]
to arrive (ab. train)	arrij	[aríj]
arrival	arritje (f)	[arítjɛ]

| to arrive by train | arrij me tren | [aríj mɛ trɛn] |
| to get on the train | hip në tren | [hip nə trén] |

to get off the train	zbres nga treni	[zbrɛs ŋa tréni]
train wreck	aksident hekurudhor (m)	[aksidént hɛkuruðór]
to derail (vi)	del nga shinat	[dɛl ŋa ʃínat]

steam locomotive	lokomotivë me avull (f)	[lokomótivə mɛ ávuɫ]
stoker, fireman	mbikëqyrës i zjarrit (m)	[mbikəcýrəs i zjárit]
firebox	furrë (f)	[fúrə]
coal	qymyr (m)	[cymýr]

26. Ship

| ship | anije (f) | [aníjɛ] |
| vessel | mjet lundrues (m) | [mjét lundrúɛs] |

steamship	anije me avull (f)	[aníjɛ mɛ ávuɫ]
riverboat	anije lumi (f)	[aníjɛ lúmi]
cruise ship	krocierë (f)	[krotsiérə]
cruiser	anije luftarake (f)	[aníjɛ luftarákɛ]

yacht	jaht (m)	[jáht]
tugboat	anije rimorkiuese (f)	[aníjɛ rimorkiúɛsɛ]
barge	anije transportuese (f)	[aníjɛ transportúɛsɛ]
ferry	traget (m)	[tragét]

| sailing ship | anije me vela (f) | [aníjɛ mɛ véla] |
| brigantine | brigantinë (f) | [brigantínə] |

| ice breaker | akullthyese (f) | [akuɫθýɛsɛ] |
| submarine | nëndetëse (f) | [nəndétəsɛ] |

boat (flat-bottomed ~)	barkë (f)	[bárkə]
dinghy	gomone (f)	[gomónɛ]
lifeboat	varkë shpëtimi (f)	[várkə ʃpətími]
motorboat	skaf (m)	[skaf]

captain	kapiten (m)	[kapitén]
seaman	marinar (m)	[marinár]
sailor	marinar (m)	[marinár]
crew	ekip (m)	[ɛkíp]

boatswain	kryemarinar (m)	[kryɛmarinár]
ship's boy	djali i anijes (m)	[djáli i aníjɛs]
cook	kuzhinier (m)	[kuʒiniér]
ship's doctor	doktori i anijes (m)	[doktóri i aníjɛs]

deck	kuverta (f)	[kuvérta]
mast	direk (m)	[dirék]
sail	vela (f)	[véla]
hold	bagazh (m)	[bagáʒ]
bow (prow)	harku sipëror (m)	[hárku sipərór]

stern	**pjesa e pasme** (f)	[pjésa ɛ pásmɛ]
oar	**rrem** (m)	[rɛm]
screw propeller	**helikë** (f)	[hɛlíkə]

cabin	**kabinë** (f)	[kabínə]
wardroom	**zyrë e oficerëve** (m)	[zýrə ɛ ofitsérəvɛ]
engine room	**salla e motorit** (m)	[sáɫa ɛ motórit]
bridge	**urë komanduese** (f)	[úrə komandúɛsɛ]
radio room	**kabina radiotelegrafike** (f)	[kabína radiotɛlɛgrafíkɛ]
wave (radio)	**valë** (f)	[válə]
logbook	**libri i shënimeve** (m)	[líbri i ʃənímɛvɛ]

spyglass	**dylbi** (f)	[dylbí]
bell	**këmbanë** (f)	[kəmbánə]
flag	**flamur** (m)	[flamúr]

hawser (mooring ~)	**pallamar** (m)	[paɫamár]
knot (bowline, etc.)	**nyjë** (f)	[nýjə]

deckrails	**parmakë** (pl)	[parmákə]
gangway	**shkallë** (f)	[ʃkáɫə]

anchor	**spirancë** (f)	[spirántsə]
to weigh anchor	**ngre spirancën**	[ŋré spirántsən]
to drop anchor	**hedh spirancën**	[hɛð spirántsən]
anchor chain	**zinxhir i spirancës** (m)	[zindʒír i spirántsəs]

port (harbor)	**port** (m)	[port]
quay, wharf	**skelë** (f)	[skélə]
to berth (moor)	**ankoroj**	[ankorój]
to cast off	**niset**	[nísɛt]

trip, voyage	**udhëtim** (m)	[uðətím]
cruise (sea trip)	**udhëtim me krocierë** (f)	[uðətím mɛ krotsiérə]
course (route)	**kursi i udhëtimit** (m)	[kúrsi i uðətímit]
route (itinerary)	**itinerar** (m)	[itinɛrár]

fairway (safe water channel)	**ujëra të lundrueshme** (f)	[újəra tə lundrúɛʃmɛ]
shallows	**cekëtinë** (f)	[tsɛkətínə]
to run aground	**bllokohet në rërë**	[bɫokóhɛt nə rərə]

storm	**stuhi** (f)	[stuhí]
signal	**sinjal** (m)	[siɲál]
to sink (vi)	**fundoset**	[fundósɛt]
Man overboard!	**Njeri në det!**	[ɲɛrí nə dɛt!]
SOS (distress signal)	**SOS** (m)	[sos]
ring buoy	**bovë shpëtuese** (f)	[bóvə ʃpətúɛsɛ]

T&P BOOKS

CITY

T&P Books Publishing

bus	**autobus** (m)	[autobús]
streetcar	**tramvaj** (m)	[tramváj]
trolley bus	**autobus tramvaj** (m)	[autobús tramváj]
route (of bus, etc.)	**itinerar** (m)	[itinɛrár]
number (e.g., bus ~)	**numër** (m)	[númər]
to go by ...	**udhëtoj me ...**	[uðətój mɛ ...]
to get on (~ the bus)	**hip**	[hip]
to get off ...	**zbres ...**	[zbrɛs ...]
stop (e.g., bus ~)	**stacion** (m)	[statsión]
next stop	**stacioni tjetër** (m)	[statsióni tjétər]
terminus	**terminal** (m)	[tɛrminál]
schedule	**orar** (m)	[orár]
to wait (vt)	**pres**	[prɛs]
ticket	**biletë** (f)	[bilétə]
fare	**çmim bilete** (m)	[tʃmím bilétɛ]
cashier (ticket seller)	**shitës biletash** (m)	[ʃítəs bilétaʃ]
ticket inspection	**kontroll biletash** (m)	[kontróɫ bilétaʃ]
ticket inspector	**kontrollues biletash** (m)	[kontroɫúɛs bilétaʃ]
to be late (for ...)	**vonohem**	[vonóhɛm]
to miss (~ the train, etc.)	**humbas**	[humbás]
to be in a hurry	**nxitoj**	[ndzitój]
taxi, cab	**taksi** (m)	[táksi]
taxi driver	**shofer taksie** (m)	[ʃofér taksíɛ]
by taxi	**me taksi**	[mɛ táksi]
taxi stand	**stacion taksish** (m)	[statsión táksiʃ]
to call a taxi	**thërras taksi**	[θərás táksi]
to take a taxi	**marr taksi**	[mar táksi]
traffic	**trafik** (m)	[trafík]
traffic jam	**bllokim trafiku** (m)	[bɫokím trafíku]
rush hour	**orë e trafikut të rëndë** (f)	[órə ɛ trafíkut tə rəndə]
to park (vi)	**parkoj**	[parkój]
to park (vt)	**parkim**	[parkím]
parking lot	**parking** (m)	[parkíŋ]
subway	**metro** (f)	[mɛtró]
station	**stacion** (m)	[statsión]
to take the subway	**shkoj me metro**	[ʃkoj mɛ métro]

| train | tren (m) | [trɛn] |
| train station | stacion treni (m) | [statsión tréni] |

28. City. Life in the city

city, town	qytet (m)	[cytét]
capital city	kryeqytet (m)	[kryɛcytét]
village	fshat (m)	[fʃát]

city map	hartë e qytetit (f)	[hártə ɛ cytétit]
downtown	qendër e qytetit (f)	[céndər ɛ cytétit]
suburb	periferi (f)	[pɛrifɛrí]
suburban (adj)	periferik	[pɛrifɛrík]

outskirts	periferia (f)	[pɛrifɛría]
environs (suburbs)	periferia (f)	[pɛrifɛría]
city block	bllok pallatesh (m)	[bɫók paɫátɛʃ]
residential block (area)	bllok banimi (m)	[bɫók baními]

traffic	trafik (m)	[trafík]
traffic lights	semafor (m)	[sɛmafór]
public transportation	transport publik (m)	[transpórt publík]
intersection	kryqëzim (m)	[krycəzím]

crosswalk	kalim për këmbësorë (m)	[kalím pər kəmbəsórə]
pedestrian underpass	nënkalim për këmbësorë (m)	[nənkalím pər kəmbəsórə]
to cross (~ the street)	kapërcej	[kapərtséj]
pedestrian	këmbësor (m)	[kəmbəsór]
sidewalk	trotuar (m)	[trotuár]

bridge	urë (f)	[úrə]
embankment (river walk)	breg lumi (m)	[brɛg lúmi]
fountain	shatërvan (m)	[ʃatərván]

allée (garden walkway)	rrugëz (m)	[rúgəz]
park	park (m)	[park]
boulevard	bulevard (m)	[bulɛvárd]
square	shesh (m)	[ʃɛʃ]
avenue (wide street)	bulevard (m)	[bulɛvárd]
street	rrugë (f)	[rúgə]
side street	rrugë dytësore (f)	[rúgə dytəsórɛ]
dead end	rrugë pa krye (f)	[rúgə pa krýɛ]

house	shtëpi (f)	[ʃtəpí]
building	ndërtesë (f)	[ndərtésə]
skyscraper	qiellgërvishtës (m)	[ciɛɫgərvíʃtəs]

| facade | fasadë (f) | [fasádə] |
| roof | çati (f) | [tʃatí] |

window	dritare (f)	[dritárɛ]
arch	hark (m)	[hárk]
column	kolonë (f)	[kolónə]
corner	kënd (m)	[kǽnd]

store window	vitrinë (f)	[vitrínə]
signboard (store sign, etc.)	tabelë (f)	[tabélə]
poster (e.g., playbill)	poster (m)	[postér]
advertising poster	afishe reklamuese (f)	[afíʃɛ rɛklamúɛsɛ]
billboard	tabelë reklamash (f)	[tabélə rɛklámaʃ]

garbage, trash	plehra (f)	[pléhra]
trash can (public ~)	kosh plehrash (m)	[koʃ pléhraʃ]
to litter (vi)	hedh mbeturina	[hɛð mbɛturína]
garbage dump	deponi plehrash (f)	[dɛponí pléhraʃ]

phone booth	kabinë telefonike (f)	[kabínə tɛlɛfoníkɛ]
lamppost	shtyllë dritash (f)	[ʃtýłə drítaʃ]
bench (park ~)	stol (m)	[stol]

police officer	polic (m)	[políts]
police	polici (f)	[politsí]
beggar	lypës (m)	[lýpəs]
homeless (n)	i pastrehë (m)	[i pastréhə]

29. Urban institutions

store	dyqan (m)	[dycán]
drugstore, pharmacy	farmaci (f)	[farmatsí]
eyeglass store	optikë (f)	[optíkə]
shopping mall	qendër tregtare (f)	[céndər trɛgtárɛ]
supermarket	supermarket (m)	[supɛrmarkét]

bakery	furrë (f)	[fúrə]
baker	furrtar (m)	[furtár]
pastry shop	pastiçeri (f)	[pastitʃɛrí]
grocery store	dyqan ushqimor (m)	[dycán uʃcimór]
butcher shop	dyqan mishi (m)	[dycán míʃi]

| produce store | dyqan fruta-perimesh (m) | [dycán frúta-pɛrímɛʃ] |
| market | treg (m) | [trɛg] |

coffee house	kafene (f)	[kafɛné]
restaurant	restorant (m)	[rɛstoránt]
pub, bar	pab (m), pijetore (f)	[pab], [pijɛtórɛ]
pizzeria	piceri (f)	[pitsɛrí]

hair salon	parukeri (f)	[parukɛrí]
post office	zyrë postare (f)	[zýrə postárɛ]
dry cleaners	pastrim kimik (m)	[pastrím kimík]

photo studio	studio fotografike (f)	[stúdio fotografíkɛ]
shoe store	dyqan këpucësh (m)	[dycán kəpútsəʃ]
bookstore	librari (f)	[librarí]
sporting goods store	dyqan me mallra sportivë (m)	[dycán mɛ máɬra sportívə]
clothes repair shop	rrobaqepësi (f)	[robacɛpəsí]
formal wear rental	dyqan veshjesh me qira (m)	[dycán véʃjɛʃ mɛ cirá]
video rental store	dyqan videosh me qira (m)	[dycán vídɛoʃ mɛ cirá]
circus	cirk (m)	[tsírk]
zoo	kopsht zoologjik (m)	[kópʃt zooloɟík]
movie theater	kinema (f)	[kinɛmá]
museum	muze (m)	[muzé]
library	bibliotekë (f)	[bibliotékə]
theater	teatër (m)	[tɛátər]
opera (opera house)	opera (f)	[opéra]
nightclub	klub nate (m)	[klúb nátɛ]
casino	kazino (f)	[kazíno]
mosque	xhami (f)	[dʒamí]
synagogue	sinagogë (f)	[sinagógə]
cathedral	katedrale (f)	[katɛdrálɛ]
temple	tempull (m)	[témpuɬ]
church	kishë (f)	[kíʃə]
college	kolegj (m)	[koléɟ]
university	universitet (m)	[univɛrsitét]
school	shkollë (f)	[ʃkóɬə]
prefecture	prefekturë (f)	[prɛfɛktúrə]
city hall	bashki (f)	[baʃkí]
hotel	hotel (m)	[hotél]
bank	bankë (f)	[bánkə]
embassy	ambasadë (f)	[ambasádə]
travel agency	agjenci udhëtimesh (f)	[aɟɛntsí uðətímɛʃ]
information office	zyrë informacioni (f)	[zýrə informatsióni]
currency exchange	këmbim valutor (m)	[kəmbím valutór]
subway	metro (f)	[mɛtró]
hospital	spital (m)	[spitál]
gas station	pikë karburanti (f)	[píkə karburánti]
parking lot	parking (m)	[parkíŋ]

30. Signs

signboard (store sign, etc.)	**tabelë** (f)	[tabélə]
notice (door sign, etc.)	**njoftim** (m)	[ɲoftím]
poster	**poster** (m)	[postér]
direction sign	**tabelë drejtuese** (f)	[tabélə drɛjtúɛsɛ]
arrow (sign)	**shigjetë** (f)	[ʃiɟétə]
caution	**kujdes** (m)	[kujdés]
warning sign	**shenjë paralajmëruese** (f)	[ʃéɲə paralajmərúɛsɛ]
to warn (vt)	**paralajmëroj**	[paralajmərój]
rest day (weekly ~)	**ditë pushimi** (f)	[dítə puʃími]
timetable (schedule)	**orar** (m)	[orár]
opening hours	**orari i punës** (m)	[orári i púnəs]
WELCOME!	**MIRË SE VINI!**	[mírə sɛ víni!]
ENTRANCE	**HYRJE**	[hýrjɛ]
EXIT	**DALJE**	[dáljɛ]
PUSH	**SHTY**	[ʃty]
PULL	**TËRHIQ**	[tərhíc]
OPEN	**HAPUR**	[hápur]
CLOSED	**MBYLLUR**	[mbýłur]
WOMEN	**GRA**	[gra]
MEN	**BURRA**	[búra]
DISCOUNTS	**ZBRITJE**	[zbrítjɛ]
SALE	**ULJE**	[úljɛ]
NEW!	**TË REJA!**	[tə réja!]
FREE	**FALAS**	[fálas]
ATTENTION!	**KUJDES!**	[kujdés!]
NO VACANCIES	**NUK KA VENDE TË LIRA**	[nuk ka véndɛ tə líra]
RESERVED	**E REZERVUAR**	[ɛ rɛzɛrvúar]
ADMINISTRATION	**ADMINISTRATA**	[administráta]
STAFF ONLY	**VETËM PËR STAFIN**	[vétəm pər stáfin]
BEWARE OF THE DOG!	**RUHUNI NGA QENI!**	[rúhuni ŋa céni!]
NO SMOKING	**NDALOHET DUHANI**	[ndalóhɛt duháni]
DO NOT TOUCH!	**MOS PREK!**	[mos prék!]
DANGEROUS	**TË RREZIKSHME**	[tə rɛzíkʃmɛ]
DANGER	**RREZIK**	[rɛzík]
HIGH VOLTAGE	**TENSION I LARTË**	[tɛnsión i lártə]
NO SWIMMING!	**NUK LEJOHET NOTI!**	[nuk lɛjóhɛt nóti!]
OUT OF ORDER	**E PRISHUR**	[ɛ príʃur]
FLAMMABLE	**LËNDË DJEGËSE**	[ləndə djégəsɛ]
FORBIDDEN	**E NDALUAR**	[ɛ ndalúar]

| NO TRESPASSING! | NDALOHET HYRJA | [ndalóhɛt hýrja] |
| WET PAINT | BOJË E FRESKËT | [bójə ɛ frésкət] |

31. Shopping

to buy (purchase)	blej	[blɛj]
purchase	blerje (f)	[blérjɛ]
to go shopping	shkoj për pazar	[ʃkoj pər pazár]
shopping	pazar (m)	[pazár]

| to be open (ab. store) | hapur | [hápur] |
| to be closed | mbyllur | [mbýɫur] |

footwear, shoes	këpucë (f)	[kəpútsə]
clothes, clothing	veshje (f)	[véʃɛ]
cosmetics	kozmetikë (f)	[kozmɛtíkə]
food products	mallra ushqimore (f)	[máɫra uʃcimórɛ]
gift, present	dhuratë (f)	[ðurátə]

| salesman | shitës (m) | [ʃítəs] |
| saleswoman | shitëse (f) | [ʃítəsɛ] |

check out, cash desk	arkë (f)	[árkə]
mirror	pasqyrë (f)	[pascýrə]
counter (store ~)	banak (m)	[bának]
fitting room	dhomë prove (f)	[ðómə próvɛ]

to try on	provoj	[provój]
to fit (ab. dress, etc.)	më rri mirë	[mə ri mírə]
to like (I like …)	pëlqej	[pəlcéj]

price	çmim (m)	[tʃmím]
price tag	etiketa e çmimit (f)	[ɛtikéta ɛ tʃmímit]
to cost (vt)	kushton	[kuʃtón]
How much?	Sa?	[sa?]
discount	ulje (f)	[úljɛ]

inexpensive (adj)	jo e shtrenjtë	[jo ɛ ʃtréɲtə]
cheap (adj)	e lirë	[ɛ lírə]
expensive (adj)	i shtrenjtë	[i ʃtréɲtə]
It's expensive	Është e shtrenjtë	[əʃtə ɛ ʃtréɲtə]

rental (n)	qiramarrje (f)	[ciramárjɛ]
to rent (~ a tuxedo)	marr me qira	[mar mɛ cirá]
credit (trade credit)	kredit (m)	[krɛdít]
on credit (adv)	me kredi	[mɛ krɛdí]

BOOKS

T&P

CLOTHING & ACCESSORIES

T&P Books Publishing

32. Outerwear. Coats

clothes	**rroba** (f)	[róba]
outerwear	**veshje e sipërme** (f)	[véʃjɛ ɛ sípərmɛ]
winter clothing	**veshje dimri** (f)	[véʃjɛ dímri]
coat (overcoat)	**pallto** (f)	[páɬto]
fur coat	**gëzof** (m)	[gəzóf]
fur jacket	**xhaketë lëkure** (f)	[dʒakétə ləkúrɛ]
down coat	**xhup** (m)	[dʒup]
jacket (e.g., leather ~)	**xhaketë** (f)	[dʒakétə]
raincoat (trenchcoat, etc.)	**pardesy** (f)	[pardɛsý]
waterproof (adj)	**kundër shiut**	[kúndər ʃíut]

33. Men's & women's clothing

shirt (button shirt)	**këmishë** (f)	[kəmíʃə]
pants	**pantallona** (f)	[pantaɬóna]
jeans	**xhinse** (f)	[dʒínsɛ]
suit jacket	**xhaketë kostumi** (f)	[dʒakétə kostúmi]
suit	**kostum** (m)	[kostúm]
dress (frock)	**fustan** (m)	[fustán]
skirt	**fund** (m)	[fund]
blouse	**bluzë** (f)	[blúzə]
knitted jacket (cardigan, etc.)	**xhaketë me thurje** (f)	[dʒakétə mɛ θúrjɛ]
jacket (of woman's suit)	**xhaketë femrash** (f)	[dʒakétə fémraʃ]
T-shirt	**bluzë** (f)	[blúzə]
shorts (short trousers)	**pantallona të shkurtra** (f)	[pantaɬóna tə ʃkúrtra]
tracksuit	**tuta sportive** (f)	[túta sportívɛ]
bathrobe	**peshqir trupi** (m)	[pɛʃcír trúpi]
pajamas	**pizhame** (f)	[piʒámɛ]
sweater	**triko** (f)	[tríko]
pullover	**pulovër** (m)	[pulóvər]
vest	**jelek** (m)	[jɛlék]
tailcoat	**frak** (m)	[frak]
tuxedo	**smoking** (m)	[smokíŋ]
uniform	**uniformë** (f)	[unifórmə]
workwear	**rroba pune** (f)	[róba púnɛ]

overalls	kominoshe (f)	[kominóʃɛ]
coat (e.g., doctor's smock)	uniformë (f)	[unifórmə]

34. Clothing. Underwear

underwear	të brendshme (f)	[tə bréndʃmɛ]
boxers, briefs	boksera (f)	[bokséra]
panties	brekë (f)	[brékə]
undershirt (A-shirt)	fanellë (f)	[fanéłə]
socks	çorape (pl)	[tʃorápɛ]

nightdress	këmishë nate (f)	[kəmíʃə nátɛ]
bra	sytjena (f)	[sytjéna]
knee highs (knee-high socks)	çorape déri tek gjuri (pl)	[tʃorápɛ déri ték ɟúri]
pantyhose	geta (f)	[géta]
stockings (thigh highs)	çorape të holla (pl)	[tʃorápɛ tə hóła]
bathing suit	rrobë banje (f)	[róbə báɲɛ]

35. Headwear

hat	kapelë (f)	[kapélə]
fedora	kapelë republike (f)	[kapélə rɛpublíkɛ]
baseball cap	kapelë bejsbolli (f)	[kapélə bɛjsbółi]
flatcap	kapelë e sheshtë (f)	[kapélə ɛ ʃéʃtə]

beret	beretë (f)	[bɛrétə]
hood	kapuç (m)	[kapútʃ]
panama hat	kapelë panama (f)	[kapélə panamá]
knit cap (knitted hat)	kapuç leshi (m)	[kapútʃ léʃi]

headscarf	shami (f)	[ʃamí]
women's hat	kapelë femrash (f)	[kapélə fémraʃ]

hard hat	helmetë (f)	[hɛlmétə]
garrison cap	kapelë ushtrie (f)	[kapélə uʃtríɛ]
helmet	helmetë (f)	[hɛlmétə]

derby	kapelë derby (f)	[kapélə dérby]
top hat	kapelë cilindër (f)	[kapélə tsilíndər]

36. Footwear

footwear	këpucë (pl)	[kəpútsə]
shoes (men's shoes)	këpucë burrash (pl)	[kəpútsə búraʃ]
shoes (women's shoes)	këpucë grash (pl)	[kəpútsə gráʃ]

boots (e.g., cowboy ~)	çizme (pl)	[tʃízmɛ]
slippers	pantofla (pl)	[pantófla]
tennis shoes (e.g., Nike ~)	atlete tenisi (pl)	[atlétɛ tɛnísi]
sneakers	atlete (pl)	[atlétɛ]
(e.g., Converse ~)		
sandals	sandale (pl)	[sandálɛ]
cobbler (shoe repairer)	këpucëtar (m)	[kəputsətár]
heel	takë (f)	[tákə]
pair (of shoes)	palë (f)	[pálə]
shoestring	lidhëse këpucësh (f)	[líðəsɛ kəpútsəʃ]
to lace (vt)	lidh këpucët	[lið kəpútsət]
shoehorn	lugë këpucësh (f)	[lúgə kəpútsəʃ]
shoe polish	bojë këpucësh (f)	[bójə kəpútsəʃ]

37. Personal accessories

gloves	dorëza (pl)	[dórəza]
mittens	doreza (f)	[doréza]
scarf (muffler)	shall (m)	[ʃaɫ]
glasses (eyeglasses)	syze (f)	[sýzɛ]
frame (eyeglass ~)	skelet syzesh (m)	[skɛlét sýzɛʃ]
umbrella	çadër (f)	[tʃádər]
walking stick	bastun (m)	[bastún]
hairbrush	furçë flokësh (f)	[fúrtʃə flókəʃ]
fan	erashkë (f)	[ɛráʃkə]
tie (necktie)	kravatë (f)	[kravátə]
bow tie	papion (m)	[papión]
suspenders	aski (pl)	[askí]
handkerchief	shami (f)	[ʃamí]
comb	krehër (m)	[kréhər]
barrette	kapëse flokësh (f)	[kápəsɛ flókəʃ]
hairpin	karficë (f)	[karfítsə]
buckle	tokëz (f)	[tókəz]
belt	rrip (m)	[rip]
shoulder strap	rrip supi (m)	[rip súpi]
bag (handbag)	çantë dore (f)	[tʃántə dórɛ]
purse	çantë (f)	[tʃántə]
backpack	çantë shpine (f)	[tʃántə ʃpínɛ]

38. Clothing. Miscellaneous

fashion	modë (f)	[módə]
in vogue (adj)	në modë	[nə módə]
fashion designer	stilist (m)	[stilíst]
collar	jakë (f)	[jákə]
pocket	xhep (m)	[dʒɛp]
pocket (as adj)	i xhepit	[i dʒépit]
sleeve	mëngë (f)	[mə́ŋə]
hanging loop	hallkë për varje (f)	[hátkə pər várjɛ]
fly (on trousers)	zinxhir (m)	[zindʒír]
zipper (fastener)	zinxhir (m)	[zindʒír]
fastener	kapëse (f)	[kápəsɛ]
button	kopsë (f)	[kópsə]
buttonhole	vrimë kopse (f)	[vrímə kópsɛ]
to come off (ab. button)	këputet	[kəpútɛt]
to sew (vi, vt)	qep	[cɛp]
to embroider (vi, vt)	qëndis	[cəndís]
embroidery	qëndisje (f)	[cəndísjɛ]
sewing needle	gjilpërë për qepje (f)	[ɟilpə́rə pər cépjɛ]
thread	pe (m)	[pɛ]
seam	tegel (m)	[tɛgél]
to get dirty (vi)	bëhem pis	[bə́hɛm pis]
stain (mark, spot)	njollë (f)	[ɲótə]
to crease, crumple (vi)	zhubros	[ʒubrós]
to tear, to rip (vt)	gris	[gris]
clothes moth	molë rrobash (f)	[mólə róbaʃ]

39. Personal care. Cosmetics

toothpaste	pastë dhëmbësh (f)	[pástə ðémbəʃ]
toothbrush	furçë dhëmbësh (f)	[fúrtʃə ðémbəʃ]
to brush one's teeth	laj dhëmbët	[laj ðémbət]
razor	brisk (m)	[brísk]
shaving cream	pastë rroje (f)	[pástə rójɛ]
to shave (vi)	rruhem	[rúhɛm]
soap	sapun (m)	[sapún]
shampoo	shampo (f)	[ʃampó]
scissors	gërshërë (f)	[gərʃérə]
nail file	limë thonjsh (f)	[límə θóɲʃ]
nail clippers	prerëse thonjsh (f)	[prérəsɛ θóɲʃ]
tweezers	piskatore vetullash (f)	[piskatórɛ vétutaʃ]

cosmetics	kozmetikë (f)	[kozmɛtíkə]
face mask	maskë fytyre (f)	[máskə fytýrɛ]
manicure	manikyr (m)	[manikýr]
to have a manicure	bëj manikyr	[bəj manikýr]
pedicure	pedikyr (m)	[pɛdikýr]

make-up bag	çantë kozmetike (f)	[tʃántə kozmɛtíkɛ]
face powder	pudër fytyre (f)	[púdər fytýrɛ]
powder compact	pudër kompakte (f)	[púdər kompáktɛ]
blusher	ruzh (m)	[ruʒ]

perfume (bottled)	parfum (m)	[parfúm]
toilet water (lotion)	parfum (m)	[parfúm]
lotion	krem (m)	[krɛm]
cologne	kolonjë (f)	[kolóɲə]

eyeshadow	rimel (m)	[rimél]
eyeliner	laps për sy (m)	[láps pər sy]
mascara	rimel (m)	[rimél]

lipstick	buzëkuq (m)	[buzəkúc]
nail polish, enamel	llak për thonj (m)	[ɬak pər θóɲ]
hair spray	llak flokësh (m)	[ɬak flókəʃ]
deodorant	deodorant (m)	[dɛodoránt]

cream	krem (m)	[krɛm]
face cream	krem për fytyrë (m)	[krɛm pər fytýrə]
hand cream	krem për duar (m)	[krɛm pər dúar]
anti-wrinkle cream	krem kundër rrudhave (m)	[krɛm kúndər rúðavɛ]
day cream	krem dite (m)	[krɛm dítɛ]
night cream	krem nate (m)	[krɛm nátɛ]
day (as adj)	dite	[dítɛ]
night (as adj)	nate	[nátɛ]

tampon	tampon (m)	[tampón]
toilet paper (toilet roll)	letër higjienike (f)	[létər hiɟiɛníkɛ]
hair dryer	tharëse flokësh (f)	[θárəsɛ flókəʃ]

40. Watches. Clocks

watch (wristwatch)	orë dore (f)	[órə dórɛ]
dial	faqe e orës (f)	[fácɛ ɛ órəs]
hand (of clock, watch)	akrep (m)	[akrép]
metal watch band	rrip metalik ore (m)	[rip mɛtalík órɛ]
watch strap	rrip ore (m)	[rip órɛ]

battery	bateri (f)	[batɛrí]
to be dead (battery)	e shkarkuar	[ɛ ʃkarkúar]
to change a battery	ndërroj baterinë	[ndərój batɛrínə]
to run fast	kalon shpejt	[kalón ʃpéjt]

to run slow	**ngel prapa**	[ŋɛl prápa]
wall clock	**orë muri** (f)	[órə múri]
hourglass	**orë rëre** (f)	[órə rərɛ]
sundial	**orë diellore** (f)	[órə diɛtórɛ]
alarm clock	**orë me zile** (f)	[órə mɛ zílɛ]
watchmaker	**orëndreqës** (m)	[orəndrécəs]
to repair (vt)	**ndreq**	[ndréc]

T&P BOOKS

EVERYDAY EXPERIENCE

T&P Books Publishing

money	**para** (f)	[pará]
currency exchange	**këmbim valutor** (m)	[kəmbím valutór]
exchange rate	**kurs këmbimi** (m)	[kurs kəmbími]
ATM	**bankomat** (m)	[bankomát]
coin	**monedhë** (f)	[monéðə]
dollar	**dollar** (m)	[doɫár]
euro	**euro** (f)	[éuro]
lira	**lirë** (f)	[lírə]
Deutschmark	**Marka gjermane** (f)	[márka ɟɛrmánɛ]
franc	**franga** (f)	[fráŋa]
pound sterling	**sterlina angleze** (f)	[stɛrlína aŋlézɛ]
yen	**jen** (m)	[jén]
debt	**borxh** (m)	[bórdʒ]
debtor	**debitor** (m)	[dɛbitór]
to lend (money)	**jap hua**	[jap huá]
to borrow (vi, vt)	**marr hua**	[mar huá]
bank	**bankë** (f)	[bánkə]
account	**llogari** (f)	[ɫogarí]
to deposit (vt)	**depozitoj**	[dɛpozitój]
to deposit into the account	**depozitoj në llogari**	[dɛpozitój nə ɫogarí]
to withdraw (vt)	**tërheq**	[tərhéc]
credit card	**kartë krediti** (f)	[kártə krɛdíti]
cash	**kesh** (m)	[kɛʃ]
check	**çek** (m)	[tʃɛk]
to write a check	**lëshoj një çek**	[ləʃój ɲə tʃék]
checkbook	**bllok çeqesh** (m)	[bɫók tʃécɛʃ]
wallet	**portofol** (m)	[portofól]
change purse	**kuletë** (f)	[kulétə]
safe	**kasafortë** (f)	[kasafórtə]
heir	**trashëgimtar** (m)	[traʃəgimtár]
inheritance	**trashëgimi** (f)	[traʃəgimí]
fortune (wealth)	**pasuri** (f)	[pasurí]
lease	**qira** (f)	[cirá]
rent (money)	**qiraja** (f)	[cirája]
to rent (sth from sb)	**marr me qira**	[mar mɛ cirá]
price	**çmim** (m)	[tʃmím]

cost	**kosto** (f)	[kósto]
sum	**shumë** (f)	[ʃúmə]

to spend (vt)	**shpenzoj**	[ʃpɛnzój]
expenses	**shpenzime** (f)	[ʃpɛnzímɛ]
to economize (vi, vt)	**kursej**	[kurséj]
economical	**ekonomik**	[ɛkonomík]

to pay (vi, vt)	**paguaj**	[pagúaj]
payment	**pagesë** (f)	[pagésə]
change (give the ~)	**kusur** (m)	[kusúr]

tax	**taksë** (f)	[táksə]
fine	**gjobë** (f)	[ɟóbə]
to fine (vt)	**vendos gjobë**	[vɛndós ɟóbə]

42. Post. Postal service

post office	**zyrë postare** (f)	[zýrə postárɛ]
mail (letters, etc.)	**postë** (f)	[póstə]
mailman	**postier** (m)	[postiér]
opening hours	**orari i punës** (m)	[orári i púnəs]

letter	**letër** (f)	[létər]
registered letter	**letër rekomande** (f)	[létər rɛkomándɛ]
postcard	**kartolinë** (f)	[kartolínə]
telegram	**telegram** (m)	[tɛlɛgrám]
package (parcel)	**pako** (f)	[páko]
money transfer	**transfer parash** (m)	[transfér paráʃ]

to receive (vt)	**pranoj**	[pranój]
to send (vt)	**dërgoj**	[dərgój]
sending	**dërgesë** (f)	[dərgésə]
address	**adresë** (f)	[adrésə]
ZIP code	**kodi postar** (m)	[kódi postár]
sender	**dërguesi** (m)	[dərgúɛsi]
receiver	**pranues** (m)	[pranúɛs]

name (first name)	**emër** (m)	[émər]
surname (last name)	**mbiemër** (m)	[mbiémər]

postage rate	**tarifë postare** (f)	[tarífə postárɛ]
standard (adj)	**standard**	[standárd]
economical (adj)	**ekonomike**	[ɛkonomíkɛ]

weight	**peshë** (f)	[péʃə]
to weigh (~ letters)	**peshoj**	[pɛʃój]
envelope	**zarf** (m)	[zarf]
postage stamp	**pullë postare** (f)	[púɫə postárɛ]
to stamp an envelope	**vendos pullën postare**	[vɛndós púɫən postárɛ]

43. Banking

bank	**bankë** (f)	[bánkə]
branch (of bank, etc.)	**degë** (f)	[dégə]
bank clerk, consultant	**punonjës banke** (m)	[punóɲəs bánkɛ]
manager (director)	**drejtor** (m)	[drɛjtór]
bank account	**llogari bankare** (f)	[ɬogarí bankárɛ]
account number	**numër llogarie** (m)	[númər ɬogaríɛ]
checking account	**llogari rrjedhëse** (f)	[ɬogarí rjéðəsɛ]
savings account	**llogari kursimesh** (f)	[ɬogarí kursímɛʃ]
to open an account	**hap një llogari**	[hap ɲə ɬogarí]
to close the account	**mbyll një llogari**	[mbýɬ ɲə ɬogarí]
to deposit into the account	**depozitoj në llogari**	[dɛpozitój nə ɬogarí]
to withdraw (vt)	**tërheq**	[tərhéc]
deposit	**depozitë** (f)	[dɛpozítə]
to make a deposit	**kryej një depozitim**	[krýɛj ɲə dɛpozitím]
wire transfer	**transfer bankar** (m)	[transfér bankár]
to wire, to transfer	**transferoj para**	[transfɛrój pará]
sum	**shumë** (f)	[ʃúmə]
How much?	**Sa?**	[sa?]
signature	**nënshkrim** (m)	[nənʃkrím]
to sign (vt)	**nënshkruaj**	[nənʃkrúaj]
credit card	**kartë krediti** (f)	[kártə krɛdíti]
code (PIN code)	**kodi PIN** (m)	[kódi pin]
credit card number	**numri i kartës**	[númri i kártəs
	së kreditit (m)	sə krɛdítit]
ATM	**bankomat** (m)	[bankomát]
check	**çek** (m)	[tʃɛk]
to write a check	**lëshoj një çek**	[ləʃój ɲə tʃék]
checkbook	**bllok çeqesh** (m)	[bɬók tʃécɛʃ]
loan (bank ~)	**kredi** (f)	[krɛdí]
to apply for a loan	**aplikoj për kredi**	[aplikój pər krɛdí]
to get a loan	**marr kredi**	[mar krɛdí]
to give a loan	**jap kredi**	[jap krɛdí]
guarantee	**garanci** (f)	[garantsí]

44. Telephone. Phone conversation

telephone	**telefon** (m)	[tɛlɛfón]
cell phone	**celular** (m)	[tsɛlulár]

answering machine	sekretari telefonike (f)	[sɛkrɛtarí tɛlɛfoníkɛ]
to call (by phone)	telefonoj	[tɛlɛfonój]
phone call	telefonatë (f)	[tɛlɛfonátə]

to dial a number	i bie numrit	[i bíɛ númrit]
Hello!	Përshëndetje!	[pərʃəndétjɛ!]
to ask (vt)	pyes	[pýɛs]
to answer (vi, vt)	përgjigjem	[pərɟíɟɛm]

to hear (vt)	dëgjoj	[dəɟój]
well (adv)	mirë	[mírə]
not well (adv)	jo mirë	[jo mírə]
noises (interference)	zhurmë (f)	[ʒúrmə]

receiver	marrës (m)	[márəs]
to pick up (~ the phone)	ngre telefonin	[ŋré tɛlɛfónin]
to hang up (~ the phone)	mbyll telefonin	[mbýɫ tɛlɛfónin]

busy (engaged)	i zënë	[i zénə]
to ring (ab. phone)	bie zilja	[bíɛ zílja]
telephone book	numerator telefonik (m)	[numɛratór tɛlɛfoník]

local (adj)	lokale	[lokálɛ]
local call	thirrje lokale (f)	[θírjɛ lokálɛ]
long distance (~ call)	distancë e largët	[distántsə ɛ lárɡət]
long-distance call	thirrje në distancë (f)	[θírjɛ nə distántsə]
international (adj)	ndërkombëtar	[ndərkombətár]
international call	thirrje ndërkombëtare (f)	[θírjɛ ndərkombətárɛ]

45. Cell phone

cell phone	celular (m)	[tsɛlulár]
display	ekran (m)	[ɛkrán]
button	buton (m)	[butón]
SIM card	karta SIM (m)	[kárta sim]

battery	bateri (f)	[batɛrí]
to be dead (battery)	e shkarkuar	[ɛ ʃkarkúar]
charger	karikues (m)	[karikúɛs]
menu	menu (f)	[mɛnú]
settings	parametra (f)	[paramétra]
tune (melody)	melodi (f)	[mɛlodí]
to select (vt)	përzgjedh	[pərzɟéð]

calculator	makinë llogaritëse (f)	[makínə ɫoɡarítəsɛ]
voice mail	postë zanore (f)	[póstə zanórɛ]
alarm clock	alarm (m)	[alárm]
contacts	kontakte (pl)	[kontáktɛ]
SMS (text message)	SMS (m)	[ɛsɛmɛs]
subscriber	abonent (m)	[abonént]

46. Stationery

ballpoint pen	stilolaps (m)	[stiloláps]
fountain pen	stilograf (m)	[stilográf]
pencil	laps (m)	[láps]
highlighter	shënjues (m)	[ʃəɲúɛs]
felt-tip pen	tushë me bojë (f)	[túʃə mɛ bójə]
notepad	bllok shënimesh (m)	[bɫók ʃənímɛʃ]
agenda (diary)	agjendë (f)	[aɟéndə]
ruler	vizore (f)	[vizórɛ]
calculator	makinë llogaritëse (f)	[makínə ɫogarítəsɛ]
eraser	gomë (f)	[gómə]
thumbtack	pineskë (f)	[pinéskə]
paper clip	kapëse fletësh (f)	[kápəsɛ flétəʃ]
glue	ngjitës (m)	[ɲítəs]
stapler	ngjitës metalik (m)	[ɲítəs mɛtalík]
hole punch	hapës vrimash (m)	[hápəs vrímaʃ]
pencil sharpener	mprehëse lapsash (m)	[mpréhəsɛ lápsaʃ]

47. Foreign languages

language	gjuhë (f)	[ɟúhə]
foreign (adj)	huaj	[húaj]
foreign language	gjuhë e huaj (f)	[ɟúhə ɛ húaj]
to study (vt)	studioj	[studiój]
to learn (language, etc.)	mësoj	[məsój]
to read (vi, vt)	lexoj	[lɛdzój]
to speak (vi, vt)	flas	[flas]
to understand (vt)	kuptoj	[kuptój]
to write (vt)	shkruaj	[ʃkrúaj]
fast (adv)	shpejt	[ʃpɛjt]
slowly (adv)	ngadalë	[ŋadálə]
fluently (adv)	rrjedhshëm	[rjéðʃəm]
rules	rregullat (pl)	[réguɫat]
grammar	gramatikë (f)	[gramatíkə]
vocabulary	fjalor (m)	[fjalór]
phonetics	fonetikë (f)	[fonɛtíkə]
textbook	tekst mësimor (m)	[tɛkst məsimór]
dictionary	fjalor (m)	[fjalór]
teach-yourself book	libër i mësimit autodidakt (m)	[líbər i məsímit autodidákt]

phrasebook	libër frazeologjik (m)	[líbər frazɛolojík]
cassette, tape	kasetë (f)	[kasétə]
videotape	videokasetë (f)	[vidɛokasétə]
CD, compact disc	CD (f)	[tsɛdé]
DVD	DVD (m)	[dividí]
alphabet	alfabet (m)	[alfabét]
to spell (vt)	gërmëzoj	[gərməzój]
pronunciation	shqiptim (m)	[ʃciptím]
accent	aksent (m)	[aksént]
with an accent	me aksent	[mɛ aksént]
without an accent	pa aksent	[pa aksént]
word	fjalë (f)	[fjálə]
meaning	kuptim (m)	[kuptím]
course (e.g., a French ~)	kurs (m)	[kurs]
to sign up	regjistrohem	[rɛjistróhɛm]
teacher	mësues (m)	[məsúɛs]
translation (process)	përkthim (m)	[pərkθím]
translation (text, etc.)	përkthim (m)	[pərkθím]
translator	përkthyes (m)	[pərkθýɛs]
interpreter	përkthyes (m)	[pərkθýɛs]
polyglot	poliglot (m)	[poliglót]
memory	kujtesë (f)	[kujtésə]

MEALS. RESTAURANT

T&P Books Publishing

48. Table setting

spoon	lugë (f)	[lúgə]
knife	thikë (f)	[θíkə]
fork	pirun (m)	[pirún]

cup (e.g., coffee ~)	filxhan (m)	[fildʒán]
plate (dinner ~)	pjatë (f)	[pjátə]
saucer	pjatë filxhani (f)	[pjátə fildʒáni]
napkin (on table)	pecetë (f)	[pɛtsétə]
toothpick	kruajtëse dhëmbësh (f)	[krúajtəsɛ ðə́mbəʃ]

49. Restaurant

restaurant	restorant (m)	[rɛstoránt]
coffee house	kafene (f)	[kafɛné]
pub, bar	pab (m), pijetore (f)	[pab], [pijɛtórɛ]
tearoom	çajtore (f)	[tʃajtórɛ]

waiter	kamerier (m)	[kamɛriér]
waitress	kameriere (f)	[kamɛriérɛ]
bartender	banakier (m)	[banakiér]
menu	menu (f)	[mɛnú]
wine list	menu verërash (f)	[mɛnú vérəraʃ]
to book a table	rezervoj një tavolinë	[rɛzɛrvój ɲə tavolínə]
course, dish	pjatë (f)	[pjátə]
to order (meal)	porosis	[porosís]
to make an order	bëj porosinë	[bəj porosínə]

aperitif	aperitiv (m)	[apɛritív]
appetizer	antipastë (f)	[antipástə]
dessert	ëmbëlsirë (f)	[əmbəlsírə]

check	faturë (f)	[fatúrə]
to pay the check	paguaj faturën	[pagúaj fatúrən]
to give change	jap kusur	[jap kusúr]
tip	bakshish (m)	[bakʃíʃ]

50. Meals

| food | ushqim (m) | [uʃcím] |
| to eat (vi, vt) | ha | [ha] |

breakfast	mëngjes (m)	[mənɟés]
to have breakfast	ha mëngjes	[ha mənɟés]
lunch	drekë (f)	[drékə]
to have lunch	ha drekë	[ha drékə]
dinner	darkë (f)	[dárkə]
to have dinner	ha darkë	[ha dárkə]

| appetite | oreks (m) | [oréks] |
| Enjoy your meal! | Të bëftë mirë! | [tə bəftə mírə!] |

to open (~ a bottle)	hap	[hap]
to spill (liquid)	derdh	[dérð]
to spill out (vi)	derdhje	[dérðjɛ]

to boil (vi)	ziej	[zíɛj]
to boil (vt)	ziej	[zíɛj]
boiled (~ water)	i zier	[i zíɛr]
to chill, cool down (vt)	ftoh	[ftoh]
to chill (vi)	ftohje	[ftóhjɛ]

| taste, flavor | shije (f) | [ʃíjɛ] |
| aftertaste | shije (f) | [ʃíjɛ] |

to slim down (lose weight)	dobësohem	[dobəsóhɛm]
diet	dietë (f)	[diétə]
vitamin	vitaminë (f)	[vitamínə]
calorie	kalori (f)	[kalorí]
vegetarian (n)	vegjetarian (m)	[vɛɟɛtarián]
vegetarian (adj)	vegjetarian	[vɛɟɛtarián]

fats (nutrient)	yndyrë (f)	[yndýrə]
proteins	proteinë (f)	[protɛínə]
carbohydrates	karbohidrat (m)	[karbohidrát]

slice (of lemon, ham)	fetë (f)	[fétə]
piece (of cake, pie)	copë (f)	[tsópə]
crumb	dromcë (f)	[drómtsə]
(of bread, cake, etc.)		

51. Cooked dishes

course, dish	pjatë (f)	[pjátə]
cuisine	kuzhinë (f)	[kuʒínə]
recipe	recetë (f)	[rɛtsétə]
portion	racion (m)	[ratsión]

salad	sallatë (f)	[saɫátə]
soup	supë (f)	[súpə]
clear soup (broth)	lëng mishi (m)	[lən míʃi]
sandwich (bread)	sandviç (m)	[sandvítʃ]

fried eggs	vezë të skuqura (pl)	[vézə tə skúcura]
hamburger (beefburger)	hamburger	[hamburgér]
beefsteak	biftek (m)	[bifték]

side dish	garniturë (f)	[garnitúrə]
spaghetti	shpageti (pl)	[ʃpagéti]
mashed potatoes	pure patatesh (f)	[puré patátɛʃ]
pizza	pica (f)	[pítsa]
porridge (oatmeal, etc.)	qull (m)	[cuɫ]
omelet	omëletë (f)	[oməlétə]

boiled (e.g., ~ beef)	i zier	[i zíɛr]
smoked (adj)	i tymosur	[i tymósur]
fried (adj)	i skuqur	[i skúcur]
dried (adj)	i tharë	[i θárə]
frozen (adj)	i ngrirë	[i ŋrírə]
pickled (adj)	i marinuar	[i marinúar]

sweet (sugary)	i ëmbël	[i ə́mbəl]
salty (adj)	i kripur	[i krípur]
cold (adj)	i ftohtë	[i ftóhtə]
hot (adj)	i nxehtë	[i ndzéhtə]
bitter (adj)	i hidhur	[i híður]
tasty (adj)	i shijshëm	[i ʃíjʃəm]

to cook in boiling water	ziej	[zíɛj]
to cook (dinner)	gatuaj	[gatúaj]
to fry (vt)	skuq	[skuc]
to heat up (food)	ngroh	[ŋróh]

to salt (vt)	hedh kripë	[hɛð krípə]
to pepper (vt)	hedh piper	[hɛð pipér]
to grate (vt)	rendoj	[rɛndój]
peel (n)	lëkurë (f)	[ləkúrə]
to peel (vt)	qëroj	[cərój]

52. Food

meat	mish (m)	[miʃ]
chicken	pulë (f)	[púlə]
Rock Cornish hen (poussin)	mish pule (m)	[miʃ púlɛ]
duck	rosë (f)	[rósə]
goose	patë (f)	[pátə]
game	gjah (m)	[ɟáh]
turkey	mish gjel deti (m)	[miʃ ɟɛl déti]

pork	mish derri (m)	[miʃ déri]
veal	mish viçi (m)	[miʃ vítʃi]
lamb	mish qengji (m)	[miʃ cénɟi]

| beef | mish lope (m) | [miʃ lópɛ] |
| rabbit | mish lepuri (m) | [miʃ lépuri] |

| sausage (bologna, etc.) | salsiçe (f) | [salsítʃɛ] |
| vienna sausage (frankfurter) | salsiçe vjeneze (f) | [salsítʃɛ vjɛnézɛ] |

bacon	proshutë (f)	[proʃútə]
ham	sallam (m)	[saɫám]
gammon	kofshë derri (f)	[kófʃə déri]

pâté	pate (f)	[paté]
liver	mëlçi (f)	[məltʃí]
hamburger (ground beef)	hamburger (m)	[hamburgér]
tongue	gjuhë (f)	[ɟúhə]

egg	ve (f)	[vɛ]
eggs	vezë (pl)	[vézə]
egg white	e bardhë veze (f)	[ɛ bárðə vézɛ]
egg yolk	e verdhë veze (f)	[ɛ vérðə vézɛ]

fish	peshk (m)	[pɛʃk]
seafood	fruta deti (pl)	[frúta déti]
crustaceans	krustace (pl)	[krustátsɛ]
caviar	havjar (m)	[havjár]

crab	gaforre (f)	[gafórɛ]
shrimp	karkalec (m)	[karkaléts]
oyster	midhje (f)	[míðjɛ]
spiny lobster	karavidhe (f)	[karavíðɛ]
octopus	oktapod (m)	[oktapód]
squid	kallamarë (f)	[kaɫamárə]

sturgeon	bli (m)	[blí]
salmon	salmon (m)	[salmón]
halibut	shojzë e Atlantikut Verior (f)	[ʃójzə ɛ atlantíkut vɛriór]

cod	merluc (m)	[mɛrlúts]
mackerel	skumbri (m)	[skúmbri]
tuna	tunë (f)	[túnə]
eel	ngjalë (f)	[ɲɟálə]

trout	troftë (f)	[tróftə]
sardine	sardele (f)	[sardélɛ]
pike	mlysh (m)	[mlýʃ]
herring	harengë (f)	[haréŋə]

bread	bukë (f)	[búkə]
cheese	djath (m)	[djáθ]
sugar	sheqer (m)	[ʃɛcér]
salt	kripë (f)	[krípə]
rice	oriz (m)	[oríz]

| pasta (macaroni) | makarona (f) | [makaróna] |
| noodles | makarona petë (f) | [makaróna pétə] |

butter	gjalp (m)	[ɟalp]
vegetable oil	vaj vegjetal (m)	[vaj vɛɟɛtál]
sunflower oil	vaj luledielli (m)	[vaj lulɛdiéłi]
margarine	margarinë (f)	[margarínə]

| olives | ullinj (pl) | [ułíɲ] |
| olive oil | vaj ulliri (m) | [vaj ułíri] |

milk	qumësht (m)	[cúməʃt]
condensed milk	qumësht i kondensuar (m)	[cúməʃt i kondɛnsúar]
yogurt	kos (m)	[kos]
sour cream	salcë kosi (f)	[sáltsə kosi]
cream (of milk)	krem qumështi (m)	[krɛm cúməʃti]

| mayonnaise | majonezë (f) | [majonézə] |
| buttercream | krem gjalpi (m) | [krɛm ɟálpi] |

groats (barley ~, etc.)	drithëra (pl)	[dríθəra]
flour	miell (m)	[míɛł]
canned food	konserva (f)	[konsérva]

cornflakes	kornfleiks (m)	[kornfléiks]
honey	mjaltë (f)	[mjáltə]
jam	reçel (m)	[rɛtʃél]
chewing gum	çamçakëz (m)	[tʃamtʃakéz]

53. Drinks

water	ujë (m)	[újə]
drinking water	ujë i pijshëm (m)	[újə i píjʃəm]
mineral water	ujë mineral (m)	[újə minɛrál]

still (adj)	ujë natyral	[újə natyrál]
carbonated (adj)	ujë i karbonuar	[újə i karbonúar]
sparkling (adj)	ujë i gazuar	[újə i gazúar]
ice	akull (m)	[ákuł]
with ice	me akull	[mɛ ákuł]

non-alcoholic (adj)	jo alkoolik	[jo alkoolík]
soft drink	pije e lehtë (f)	[píjɛ ɛ léhtə]
refreshing drink	pije freskuese (f)	[píjɛ frɛskúɛsɛ]
lemonade	limonadë (f)	[limonádə]

liquors	likere (pl)	[likérɛ]
wine	verë (f)	[vérə]
white wine	verë e bardhë (f)	[vérə ɛ bárðə]
red wine	verë e kuqe (f)	[vérə ɛ kúcɛ]

liqueur	liker (m)	[likér]
champagne	shampanjë (f)	[ʃampáɲə]
vermouth	vermut (m)	[vɛrmút]

whiskey	uiski (m)	[víski]
vodka	vodkë (f)	[vódkə]
gin	xhin (m)	[dʒin]
cognac	konjak (m)	[koɲák]
rum	rum (m)	[rum]

coffee	kafe (f)	[káfɛ]
black coffee	kafe e zezë (f)	[káfɛ ɛ zézə]
coffee with milk	kafe me qumësht (m)	[káfɛ mɛ cúməʃt]
cappuccino	kapuçino (m)	[kaputʃíno]
instant coffee	neskafe (f)	[nɛskáfɛ]

milk	qumësht (m)	[cúməʃt]
cocktail	koktej (m)	[koktéj]
milkshake	milkshake (f)	[milkʃákɛ]

juice	lëng frutash (m)	[ləŋ frútaʃ]
tomato juice	lëng domatesh (m)	[ləŋ domátɛʃ]
orange juice	lëng portokalli (m)	[ləŋ portokáɫi]
freshly squeezed juice	lëng frutash i freskët (m)	[ləŋ frútaʃ i fréskət]

beer	birrë (f)	[bírə]
light beer	birrë e lehtë (f)	[bírə ɛ léhtə]
dark beer	birrë e zezë (f)	[bírə ɛ zézə]

tea	çaj (m)	[tʃáj]
black tea	çaj i zi (m)	[tʃáj i zí]
green tea	çaj jeshil (m)	[tʃáj jɛʃíl]

54. Vegetables

| vegetables | perime (pl) | [pɛrímɛ] |
| greens | zarzavate (pl) | [zarzavátɛ] |

tomato	domate (f)	[domátɛ]
cucumber	kastravec (m)	[kastravéts]
carrot	karotë (f)	[karótə]
potato	patate (f)	[patátɛ]
onion	qepë (f)	[cépə]
garlic	hudhër (f)	[húðər]

cabbage	lakër (f)	[lákər]
cauliflower	lulelakër (f)	[lulɛlákər]
Brussels sprouts	lakër Brukseli (f)	[lákər brukséli]
broccoli	brokoli (m)	[brókoli]
beet	panxhar (m)	[pandʒár]

eggplant	patëllxhan (m)	[patəłdʒán]
zucchini	kungulleshë (m)	[kuŋułéʃə]
pumpkin	kungull (m)	[kúŋuł]
turnip	rrepë (f)	[répə]

parsley	majdanoz (m)	[majdanóz]
dill	kopër (f)	[kópər]
lettuce	sallatë jeshile (f)	[sałátə jɛʃílɛ]
celery	selino (f)	[sɛlíno]
asparagus	asparagus (m)	[asparágus]
spinach	spinaq (m)	[spinác]

pea	bizele (f)	[bizélɛ]
beans	fasule (f)	[fasúlɛ]
corn (maize)	misër (m)	[mísər]
kidney bean	groshë (f)	[gróʃə]

bell pepper	spec (m)	[spɛts]
radish	rrepkë (f)	[répkə]
artichoke	angjinare (f)	[anɟinárɛ]

55. Fruits. Nuts

fruit	frut (m)	[frut]
apple	mollë (f)	[mółə]
pear	dardhë (f)	[dárðə]
lemon	limon (m)	[limón]
orange	portokall (m)	[portokáł]
strawberry (garden ~)	luleshtrydhe (f)	[lulɛʃtrýðɛ]

mandarin	mandarinë (f)	[mandarínə]
plum	kumbull (f)	[kúmbuł]
peach	pjeshkë (f)	[pjéʃkə]
apricot	kajsi (f)	[kajsí]
raspberry	mjedër (f)	[mjédər]
pineapple	ananas (m)	[ananás]

banana	banane (f)	[banánɛ]
watermelon	shalqi (m)	[ʃalcí]
grape	rrush (m)	[ruʃ]
sour cherry	qershi vishnje (f)	[cɛrʃí víʃɲɛ]
sweet cherry	qershi (f)	[cɛrʃí]
melon	pjepër (m)	[pjépər]

grapefruit	grejpfrut (m)	[grɛjpfrút]
avocado	avokado (f)	[avokádo]
papaya	papaja (f)	[papája]
mango	mango (f)	[máɲo]
pomegranate	shegë (f)	[ʃégə]
redcurrant	kaliboba e kuqe (f)	[kalibóba ɛ kúcɛ]

blackcurrant	kaliboba e zezë (f)	[kalibóba ɛ zézə]
gooseberry	kulumbri (f)	[kulumbrí]
bilberry	boronicë (f)	[boronítsə]
blackberry	manaferra (f)	[manaféra]

raisin	rrush i thatë (m)	[ruʃ i θátə]
fig	fik (m)	[fik]
date	hurmë (f)	[húrmə]

peanut	kikirik (m)	[kikirík]
almond	bajame (f)	[bajámɛ]
walnut	arrë (f)	[árə]
hazelnut	lajthi (f)	[lajθí]
coconut	arrë kokosi (f)	[árə kokósi]
pistachios	fëstëk (m)	[fəstёk]

56. Bread. Candy

bakers' confectionery (pastry)	ëmbëlsira (pl)	[əmbəlsíra]
bread	bukë (f)	[búkə]
cookies	biskota (pl)	[biskóta]

chocolate (n)	çokollatë (f)	[tʃokoɫátə]
chocolate (as adj)	prej çokollate	[prɛj tʃokoɫátɛ]
candy (wrapped)	karamele (f)	[karamélɛ]
cake (e.g., cupcake)	kek (m)	[kék]
cake (e.g., birthday ~)	tortë (f)	[tórtə]

| pie (e.g., apple ~) | tortë (f) | [tórtə] |
| filling (for cake, pie) | mbushje (f) | [mbúʃɛ] |

jam (whole fruit jam)	reçel (m)	[rɛtʃél]
marmalade	marmelatë (f)	[marmɛlátə]
wafers	vafera (pl)	[vaféra]
ice-cream	akullore (f)	[akuɫórɛ]
pudding	puding (m)	[pudíŋ]

57. Spices

salt	kripë (f)	[krípə]
salty (adj)	i kripur	[i krípuɾ]
to salt (vt)	hedh kripë	[hɛð krípə]

black pepper	piper i zi (m)	[pipér i zi]
red pepper (milled ~)	piper i kuq (m)	[pipér i kuc]
mustard	mustardë (f)	[mustárdə]
horseradish	rrepë djegëse (f)	[répə djégəsɛ]

condiment	**salcë** (f)	[sáltsə]
spice	**erëz** (f)	[érəz]
sauce	**salcë** (f)	[sáltsə]
vinegar	**uthull** (f)	[úθuɫ]
anise	**anisetë** (f)	[anisétə]
basil	**borzilok** (m)	[borzilók]
cloves	**karafil** (m)	[karafíl]
ginger	**xhenxhefil** (m)	[dʒɛndʒɛfíl]
coriander	**koriandër** (m)	[koriándər]
cinnamon	**kanellë** (f)	[kanéɫə]
sesame	**susam** (m)	[susám]
bay leaf	**gjeth dafine** (m)	[ɟɛθ dafínɛ]
paprika	**spec** (m)	[spɛts]
caraway	**kumin** (m)	[kumín]
saffron	**shafran** (m)	[ʃafrán]

T&P BOOKS

PERSONAL INFORMATION. FAMILY

T&P Books Publishing

58. Personal information. Forms

name (first name)	**emër** (m)	[émər]
surname (last name)	**mbiemër** (m)	[mbiémər]
date of birth	**datëlindje** (f)	[datəlíndjɛ]
place of birth	**vendlindje** (f)	[vɛndlíndjɛ]
nationality	**kombësi** (f)	[kombəsí]
place of residence	**vendbanim** (m)	[vɛndbaním]
country	**shtet** (m)	[ʃtɛt]
profession (occupation)	**profesion** (m)	[profɛsión]
gender, sex	**gjinia** (f)	[ɟinía]
height	**gjatësia** (f)	[ɟatəsía]
weight	**peshë** (f)	[péʃə]

59. Family members. Relatives

mother	**nënë** (f)	[nénə]
father	**baba** (f)	[babá]
son	**bir** (m)	[bir]
daughter	**bijë** (f)	[bíjə]
younger daughter	**vajza e vogël** (f)	[vájza ɛ vógəl]
younger son	**djali i vogël** (m)	[djáli i vógəl]
eldest daughter	**vajza e madhe** (f)	[vájza ɛ máðɛ]
eldest son	**djali i vogël** (m)	[djáli i vógəl]
brother	**vëlla** (m)	[vəɫá]
elder brother	**vëllai i madh** (m)	[vəɫái i mað]
younger brother	**vëllai i vogël** (m)	[vəɫai i vógəl]
sister	**motër** (f)	[mótər]
elder sister	**motra e madhe** (f)	[mótra ɛ máðɛ]
younger sister	**motra e vogël** (f)	[mótra ɛ vógəl]
cousin (masc.)	**kushëri** (m)	[kuʃərí]
cousin (fem.)	**kushërirë** (f)	[kuʃərírə]
mom, mommy	**mami** (f)	[mámi]
dad, daddy	**babi** (m)	[bábi]
parents	**prindër** (pl)	[príndər]
child	**fëmijë** (f)	[fəmíjə]
children	**fëmijë** (pl)	[fəmíjə]
grandmother	**gjyshe** (f)	[ɟýʃɛ]

grandfather	gjysh (m)	[ɟyʃ]
grandson	nip (m)	[nip]
granddaughter	mbesë (f)	[mbésə]
grandchildren	nipër e mbesa (pl)	[nípər ɛ mbésa]

uncle	dajë (f)	[dájə]
aunt	teze (f)	[tézɛ]
nephew	nip (m)	[nip]
niece	mbesë (f)	[mbésə]
mother-in-law (wife's mother)	vjehrrë (f)	[vjéhrə]
father-in-law (husband's father)	vjehrri (m)	[vjéhri]
son-in-law (daughter's husband)	dhëndër (m)	[ðéndər]
stepmother	njerkë (f)	[ɲérkə]
stepfather	njerk (m)	[ɲérk]

infant	foshnjë (f)	[fóʃnə]
baby (infant)	fëmijë (f)	[fəmíjə]
little boy, kid	djalosh (m)	[djalóʃ]

wife	bashkëshorte (f)	[baʃkəʃórtɛ]
husband	bashkëshort (m)	[baʃkəʃórt]
spouse (husband)	bashkëshort (m)	[baʃkəʃórt]
spouse (wife)	bashkëshorte (f)	[baʃkəʃórtɛ]

married (masc.)	i martuar	[i martúar]
married (fem.)	e martuar	[ɛ martúar]
single (unmarried)	beqar	[bɛcár]
bachelor	beqar (m)	[bɛcár]
divorced (masc.)	i divorcuar	[i divortsúar]
widow	vejushë (f)	[vɛjúʃə]
widower	vejan (m)	[vɛján]

relative	kushëri (m)	[kuʃərí]
close relative	kushëri i afërt (m)	[kuʃərí i áfərt]
distant relative	kushëri i largët (m)	[kuʃərí i lárgət]
relatives	kushërinj (pl)	[kuʃəríɲ]

orphan (boy)	jetim (m)	[jɛtím]
orphan (girl)	jetime (f)	[jɛtímɛ]
guardian (of a minor)	kujdestar (m)	[kujdɛstár]
to adopt (a boy)	adoptoj	[adoptój]
to adopt (a girl)	adoptoj	[adoptój]

60. Friends. Coworkers

friend (masc.)	mik (m)	[mik]
friend (fem.)	mike (f)	[míkɛ]

| friendship | miqësi (f) | [micəsí] |
| to be friends | të miqësohem | [tə micəsóhɛm] |

buddy (masc.)	shok (m)	[ʃok]
buddy (fem.)	shoqe (f)	[ʃócɛ]
partner	partner (m)	[partnér]

chief (boss)	shef (m)	[ʃɛf]
superior (n)	epror (m)	[ɛprór]
owner, proprietor	pronar (m)	[pronár]
subordinate (n)	vartës (m)	[vártəs]
colleague	koleg (m)	[kolég]

acquaintance (person)	i njohur (m)	[i ɲóhur]
fellow traveler	bashkudhëtar (m)	[baʃkuðətár]
classmate	shok klase (m)	[ʃok klásɛ]

neighbor (masc.)	komshi (m)	[komʃí]
neighbor (fem.)	komshike (f)	[komʃíkɛ]
neighbors	komshinj (pl)	[komʃíɲ]

T&P BOOKS

HUMAN BODY.
MEDICINE

T&P Books Publishing

head	**kokë** (f)	[kókə]
face	**fytyrë** (f)	[fytýrə]
nose	**hundë** (f)	[húndə]
mouth	**gojë** (f)	[gójə]
eye	**sy** (m)	[sy]
eyes	**sytë**	[sýtə]
pupil	**bebëz** (f)	[bébəz]
eyebrow	**vetull** (f)	[vétuɫ]
eyelash	**qerpik** (m)	[cɛrpík]
eyelid	**qepallë** (f)	[cɛpáɫə]
tongue	**gjuhë** (f)	[ɟúhə]
tooth	**dhëmb** (m)	[ðəmb]
lips	**buzë** (f)	[búzə]
cheekbones	**mollëza** (f)	[móɫəza]
gum	**mishrat e dhëmbëve**	[míʃrat ɛ ðəmbəvɛ]
palate	**qiellzë** (f)	[ciéɫzə]
nostrils	**vrimat e hundës** (pl)	[vrímat ɛ húndəs]
chin	**mjekër** (f)	[mjékər]
jaw	**nofull** (f)	[nófuɫ]
cheek	**faqe** (f)	[fácɛ]
forehead	**ball** (m)	[báɫ]
temple	**tëmth** (m)	[təmθ]
ear	**vesh** (m)	[vɛʃ]
back of the head	**zverk** (m)	[zvɛrk]
neck	**qafë** (f)	[cáfə]
throat	**fyt** (m)	[fyt]
hair	**flokë** (pl)	[flókə]
hairstyle	**model flokësh** (m)	[modél flókəʃ]
haircut	**prerje flokësh** (f)	[prérjɛ flókəʃ]
wig	**paruke** (f)	[parúkɛ]
mustache	**mustaqe** (f)	[mustácɛ]
beard	**mjekër** (f)	[mjékər]
to have (a beard, etc.)	**lë mjekër**	[lə mjékər]
braid	**gërshet** (m)	[gərʃét]
sideburns	**baseta** (f)	[baséta]
red-haired (adj)	**flokëkuqe**	[flokəkúcɛ]
gray (hair)	**thinja**	[θíɲa]

| bald (adj) | qeros | [cɛrós] |
| bald patch | tullë (f) | [tútə] |

| ponytail | bishtalec (m) | [biʃtaléts] |
| bangs | balluke (f) | [batúkɛ] |

62. Human body

| hand | dorë (f) | [dórə] |
| arm | krah (m) | [krah] |

finger	gisht i dorës (m)	[gíʃt i dórəs]
toe	gisht i këmbës (m)	[gíʃt i kémbəs]
thumb	gishti i madh (m)	[gíʃti i máð]
little finger	gishti i vogël (m)	[gíʃti i vógəl]
nail	thua (f)	[θúa]

fist	grusht (m)	[grúʃt]
palm	pëllëmbë dore (f)	[pətémbə dórɛ]
wrist	kyç (m)	[kytʃ]
forearm	parakrah (m)	[parakráh]
elbow	bërryl (m)	[bərýl]
shoulder	shpatull (f)	[ʃpátut]

leg	këmbë (f)	[kémbə]
foot	shputë (f)	[ʃpútə]
knee	gju (m)	[ɟú]
calf (part of leg)	pulpë (f)	[púlpə]
hip	ijë (f)	[íjə]
heel	thembër (f)	[θémbər]

body	trup (m)	[trup]
stomach	stomak (m)	[stomák]
chest	kraharor (m)	[kraharór]
breast	gjoks (m)	[ɟóks]
flank	krah (m)	[krah]
back	kurriz (m)	[kuríz]

| lower back | fundshpina (f) | [fundʃpína] |
| waist | beli (m) | [béli] |

navel (belly button)	kërthizë (f)	[kərθízə]
buttocks	vithe (f)	[víθɛ]
bottom	prapanica (f)	[prapanítsa]

beauty mark	nishan (m)	[niʃán]
birthmark (café au lait spot)	shenjë lindjeje (f)	[ʃéɲə líndjɛjɛ]
tattoo	tatuazh (m)	[tatuáʒ]
scar	shenjë (f)	[ʃéɲə]

63. Diseases

sickness	**sëmundje** (f)	[səmúndjɛ]
to be sick	**jam sëmurë**	[jam səmúrə]
health	**shëndet** (m)	[ʃəndét]
runny nose (coryza)	**rrifë** (f)	[rífə]
tonsillitis	**grykët** (m)	[grýkət]
cold (illness)	**ftohje** (f)	[ftóhjɛ]
to catch a cold	**ftohem**	[ftóhɛm]
bronchitis	**bronkit** (m)	[bronkít]
pneumonia	**pneumoni** (f)	[pnɛumoní]
flu, influenza	**grip** (m)	[grip]
nearsighted (adj)	**miop**	[mióp]
farsighted (adj)	**presbit**	[prɛsbít]
strabismus (crossed eyes)	**strabizëm** (m)	[strabízəm]
cross-eyed (adj)	**strabik**	[strabík]
cataract	**katarakt** (m)	[katarákt]
glaucoma	**glaukoma** (f)	[glaukóma]
stroke	**goditje** (f)	[godítjɛ]
heart attack	**sulm në zemër** (m)	[sulm nə zémər]
myocardial infarction	**infarkt miokardiak** (m)	[infárkt miokardiák]
paralysis	**paralizë** (f)	[paralízə]
to paralyze (vt)	**paralizoj**	[paralizój]
allergy	**alergji** (f)	[alɛɾɟí]
asthma	**astmë** (f)	[ástmə]
diabetes	**diabet** (m)	[diabét]
toothache	**dhimbje dhëmbi** (f)	[ðímbjɛ ðə́mbi]
caries	**karies** (m)	[kariés]
diarrhea	**diarre** (f)	[diaré]
constipation	**kapsllëk** (m)	[kapsɬə́k]
stomach upset	**dispepsi** (f)	[dispɛpsí]
food poisoning	**helmim** (m)	[hɛlmím]
to get food poisoning	**helmohem nga ushqimi**	[hɛlmóhɛm ŋa uʃcími]
arthritis	**artrit** (m)	[artrít]
rickets	**rakit** (m)	[rakít]
rheumatism	**reumatizëm** (m)	[rɛumatízəm]
atherosclerosis	**arteriosklerozë** (f)	[artɛriosklɛrózə]
gastritis	**gastrit** (m)	[gastrít]
appendicitis	**apendicit** (m)	[apɛnditsít]
cholecystitis	**kolecistit** (m)	[kolɛtsistít]
ulcer	**ulcerë** (f)	[ultsérə]
measles	**fruth** (m)	[fruθ]

rubella (German measles)	rubeola (f)	[rubɛóla]
jaundice	verdhëza (f)	[vérðɛza]
hepatitis	hepatit (m)	[hɛpatít]

schizophrenia	skizofreni (f)	[skizofrɛní]
rabies (hydrophobia)	sëmundje e tërbimit (f)	[səmúndjɛ ɛ tərbímit]
neurosis	neurozë (f)	[nɛurózə]
concussion	tronditje (f)	[trondítjɛ]

cancer	kancer (m)	[kantsér]
sclerosis	sklerozë (f)	[sklɛrózə]
multiple sclerosis	sklerozë e shumëfishtë (f)	[sklɛrózə ɛ ʃuməfíʃtə]

alcoholism	alkoolizëm (m)	[alkoolízəm]
alcoholic (n)	alkoolik (m)	[alkoolík]
syphilis	sifiliz (m)	[sifilíz]
AIDS	SIDA (f)	[sída]

tumor	tumor (m)	[tumór]
malignant (adj)	malinj	[malíɲ]
benign (adj)	beninj	[bɛníɲ]

fever	ethe (f)	[éθɛ]
malaria	malarie (f)	[malaríɛ]
gangrene	gangrenë (f)	[gaŋrénə]
seasickness	sëmundje deti (f)	[səmúndjɛ déti]
epilepsy	epilepsi (f)	[ɛpilɛpsí]

epidemic	epidemi (f)	[ɛpidɛmí]
typhus	tifo (f)	[tífo]
tuberculosis	tuberkuloz (f)	[tubɛrkulóz]
cholera	kolerë (f)	[kolérə]
plague (bubonic ~)	murtaja (f)	[murtája]

64. Symptoms. Treatments. Part 1

symptom	simptomë (f)	[simptómə]
temperature	temperaturë (f)	[tɛmpɛratúrə]
high temperature (fever)	temperaturë e lartë (f)	[tɛmpɛratúrə ɛ lártə]
pulse (heartbeat)	puls (m)	[puls]

dizziness (vertigo)	marrje mendsh (m)	[márjɛ méndʃ]
hot (adj)	i nxehtë	[i ndzéhtə]
shivering	drithërima (f)	[driθəríma]
pale (e.g., ~ face)	i zbehur	[i zbéhur]

cough	kollë (f)	[kółə]
to cough (vi)	kollitem	[kołítɛm]
to sneeze (vi)	teshtij	[tɛʃtíj]
faint	të fikët (f)	[tə fíkət]

to faint (vi)	**bie të fikët**	[bíɛ tə fíkət]
bruise (hématome)	**mavijosje** (f)	[mavijósjɛ]
bump (lump)	**gungë** (f)	[gúŋə]
to bang (bump)	**godas**	[godás]
contusion (bruise)	**lëndim** (m)	[ləndím]
to get a bruise	**lëndohem**	[ləndóhɛm]
to limp (vi)	**çaloj**	[tʃalój]
dislocation	**dislokim** (m)	[dislokím]
to dislocate (vt)	**del nga vendi**	[dɛl ŋa véndi]
fracture	**thyerje** (f)	[θýɛrjɛ]
to have a fracture	**thyej**	[θýɛj]
cut (e.g., paper ~)	**e prerë** (f)	[ɛ prérə]
to cut oneself	**pres veten**	[prɛs vétɛn]
bleeding	**rrjedhje gjaku** (f)	[rjéðjɛ ɟáku]
burn (injury)	**djegie** (f)	[djégiɛ]
to get burned	**digjem**	[díɟɛm]
to prick (vt)	**shpoj**	[ʃpoj]
to prick oneself	**shpohem**	[ʃpóhɛm]
to injure (vt)	**dëmtoj**	[dəmtój]
injury	**dëmtim** (m)	[dəmtím]
wound	**plagë** (f)	[plágə]
trauma	**traumë** (f)	[traúmə]
to be delirious	**fol përçart**	[fól pərtʃárt]
to stutter (vi)	**belbëzoj**	[bɛlbəzój]
sunstroke	**pikë e diellit** (f)	[píkə ɛ diéɬit]

65. Symptoms. Treatments. Part 2

pain, ache	**dhimbje** (f)	[ðímbjɛ]
splinter (in foot, etc.)	**cifël** (f)	[tsífəl]
sweat (perspiration)	**djersë** (f)	[djérsə]
to sweat (perspire)	**djersij**	[djɛrsíj]
vomiting	**të vjella** (f)	[tə vjéɬa]
convulsions	**konvulsione** (f)	[konvulsiónɛ]
pregnant (adj)	**shtatzënë**	[ʃtatzénə]
to be born	**lind**	[lind]
delivery, labor	**lindje** (f)	[líndjɛ]
to deliver (~ a baby)	**sjell në jetë**	[sjɛɬ nə jétə]
abortion	**abort** (m)	[abórt]
breathing, respiration	**frymëmarrje** (f)	[fryməmárjɛ]
in-breath (inhalation)	**mbajtje e frymës** (f)	[mbájtjɛ ɛ frýməs]
out-breath (exhalation)	**lëshim i frymës** (m)	[ləʃím i frýməs]

| to exhale (breathe out) | nxjerr frymën | [ndzjér frýmən] |
| to inhale (vi) | marr frymë | [mar frýmə] |

disabled person	invalid (m)	[invalíd]
cripple	i gjymtuar (m)	[i ɟymtúar]
drug addict	narkoman (m)	[narkomán]

deaf (adj)	shurdh	[ʃurð]
mute (adj)	memec	[mɛméts]
deaf mute (adj)	shurdh-memec	[ʃurð-mɛméts]

mad, insane (adj)	i marrë	[i márə]
madman (demented person)	i çmendur (m)	[i tʃméndur]
madwoman	e çmendur (f)	[ɛ tʃméndur]
to go insane	çmendem	[tʃméndɛm]

gene	gen (m)	[gɛn]
immunity	imunitet (m)	[imunitét]
hereditary (adj)	e trashëguar	[ɛ traʃəgúar]
congenital (adj)	e lindur	[ɛ líndur]

virus	virus (m)	[virús]
microbe	mikrob (m)	[mikrób]
bacterium	bakterie (f)	[baktériɛ]
infection	infeksion (m)	[infɛksión]

66. Symptoms. Treatments. Part 3

| hospital | spital (m) | [spitál] |
| patient | pacient (m) | [patsiént] |

diagnosis	diagnozë (f)	[diagnózə]
cure	kurë (f)	[kúrə]
medical treatment	trajtim mjekësor (m)	[trajtím mjɛkəsór]
to get treatment	kurohem	[kuróhɛm]
to treat (~ a patient)	kuroj	[kurój]
to nurse (look after)	kujdesem	[kujdésɛm]
care (nursing ~)	kujdes (m)	[kujdés]

operation, surgery	operacion (m)	[opɛratsión]
to bandage (head, limb)	fashoj	[faʃój]
bandaging	fashim (m)	[faʃím]

vaccination	vaksinim (m)	[vaksiním]
to vaccinate (vt)	vaksinoj	[vaksinój]
injection, shot	injeksion (m)	[iɲɛksión]
to give an injection	bëj injeksion	[bəj iɲɛksíon]
attack	atak (m)	[aták]
amputation	amputim (m)	[amputím]

to amputate (vt)	amputoj	[amputój]
coma	komë (f)	[kómə]
to be in a coma	jam në komë	[jam nə kómə]
intensive care	kujdes intensiv (m)	[kujdés intɛnsív]
to recover (~ from flu)	shërohem	[ʃəróhɛm]
condition (patient's ~)	gjendje (f)	[ɟéndjɛ]
consciousness	vetëdije (f)	[vɛtədíjɛ]
memory (faculty)	kujtesë (f)	[kujtésə]
to pull out (tooth)	heq	[hɛc]
filling	mbushje (f)	[mbúʃɛ]
to fill (a tooth)	mbush	[mbúʃ]
hypnosis	hipnozë (f)	[hipnózə]
to hypnotize (vt)	hipnotizim	[hipnotizím]

67. Medicine. Drugs. Accessories

medicine, drug	ilaç (m)	[ilátʃ]
remedy	mjekim (m)	[mjɛkím]
to prescribe (vt)	shkruaj recetë	[ʃkrúaj rɛtsétə]
prescription	recetë (f)	[rɛtsétə]
tablet, pill	pilulë (f)	[pilúlə]
ointment	krem (m)	[krɛm]
ampule	ampulë (f)	[ampúlə]
mixture, solution	përzierje (f)	[pərzíɛrjɛ]
syrup	shurup (m)	[ʃurúp]
capsule	pilulë (f)	[pilúlə]
powder	pudër (f)	[púdər]
gauze bandage	fashë garze (f)	[faʃə gárzɛ]
cotton wool	pambuk (m)	[pambúk]
iodine	jod (m)	[jod]
Band-Aid	leukoplast (m)	[lɛukoplást]
eyedropper	pikatore (f)	[pikatórɛ]
thermometer	termometër (m)	[tɛrmométər]
syringe	shiringë (f)	[ʃíríŋə]
wheelchair	karrocë me rrota (f)	[karótsə mɛ róta]
crutches	paterica (f)	[patɛrítsa]
painkiller	qetësues (m)	[cɛtəsúɛs]
laxative	laksativ (m)	[laksatív]
spirits (ethanol)	alkool dezinfektues (m)	[alkoól dɛzinfɛktúɛs]
medicinal herbs	bimë mjekësore (f)	[bímə mjɛkəsórɛ]
herbal (~ tea)	çaj bimor	[tʃáj bimór]

APARTMENT

T&P Books Publishing

apartment	**apartament** (m)	[apartamént]
room	**dhomë** (f)	[ðómə]
bedroom	**dhomë gjumi** (f)	[ðómə ɟúmi]
dining room	**dhomë ngrënie** (f)	[ðómə ŋrəníɛ]
living room	**dhomë ndeje** (f)	[ðómə ndéjɛ]
study (home office)	**dhomë pune** (f)	[ðómə púnɛ]
entry room	**hyrje** (f)	[hýrjɛ]
bathroom (room with	**banjo** (f)	[báɲo]
a bath or shower)		
half bath	**tualet** (m)	[tualét]
ceiling	**tavan** (m)	[taván]
floor	**dysheme** (f)	[dyʃɛmé]
corner	**qoshe** (f)	[cóʃɛ]

furniture	**orendi** (f)	[orɛndí]
table	**tryezë** (f)	[tryézə]
chair	**karrige** (f)	[karígɛ]
bed	**shtrat** (m)	[ʃtrat]
couch, sofa	**divan** (m)	[diván]
armchair	**kolltuk** (m)	[koɫtúk]
bookcase	**raft librash** (m)	[ráft líbraʃ]
shelf	**sergjen** (m)	[sɛɟén]
wardrobe	**gardërobë** (f)	[gardəróbə]
coat rack (wall-mounted ~)	**varëse** (f)	[várəsɛ]
coat stand	**varëse xhaketash** (f)	[várəsɛ dʒakétaʃ]
bureau, dresser	**komodë** (f)	[komódə]
coffee table	**tryezë e ulët** (f)	[tryézə ɛ úlət]
mirror	**pasqyrë** (f)	[pascýrə]
carpet	**qilim** (m)	[cilím]
rug, small carpet	**tapet** (m)	[tapét]
fireplace	**oxhak** (m)	[odʒák]
candle	**qiri** (m)	[círi]
candlestick	**shandan** (m)	[ʃandán]

drapes	perde (f)	[pérdɛ]
wallpaper	tapiceri (f)	[tapitsɛrí]
blinds (jalousie)	grila (f)	[gríla]

table lamp	llambë tavoline (f)	[ɫámbə tavolínɛ]
wall lamp (sconce)	llambadar muri (m)	[ɫambadár múri]
floor lamp	llambadar (m)	[ɫambadár]
chandelier	llambadar (m)	[ɫambadár]

leg (of chair, table)	këmbë (f)	[kémbə]
armrest	mbështetëse krahu (f)	[mbəʃtétəsɛ kráhu]
back (backrest)	mbështetëse (f)	[mbəʃtétəsɛ]
drawer	sirtar (m)	[sirtár]

70. Bedding

bedclothes	çarçafë (pl)	[tʃartʃáfə]
pillow	jastëk (m)	[jasték]
pillowcase	këllëf jastëku (m)	[kəɫéf jastéku]
duvet, comforter	jorgan (m)	[jorgán]
sheet	çarçaf (m)	[tʃartʃáf]
bedspread	mbulesë (f)	[mbulésə]

71. Kitchen

kitchen	kuzhinë (f)	[kuʒínə]
gas	gaz (m)	[gaz]
gas stove (range)	sobë me gaz (f)	[sóbə mɛ gaz]
electric stove	sobë elektrike (f)	[sóbə ɛlɛktríkɛ]
oven	furrë (f)	[fúrə]
microwave oven	mikrovalë (f)	[mikroválə]

refrigerator	frigorifer (m)	[frigorifér]
freezer	frigorifer (m)	[frigorifér]
dishwasher	pjatalarëse (f)	[pjatalárəsɛ]

meat grinder	grirëse mishi (f)	[grírəsɛ míʃi]
juicer	shtrydhëse frutash (f)	[ʃtrýðəsɛ frútaʃ]
toaster	toster (m)	[tostér]
mixer	mikser (m)	[miksér]

coffee machine	makinë kafeje (f)	[makínə kaféjɛ]
coffee pot	kafetierë (f)	[kafɛtiérə]
coffee grinder	mulli kafeje (f)	[muɫí káfɛjɛ]

kettle	çajnik (m)	[tʃajník]
teapot	çajnik (m)	[tʃajník]
lid	kapak (m)	[kapák]

tea strainer	sitë çaji (f)	[sítə tʃáji]
spoon	lugë (f)	[lúgə]
teaspoon	lugë çaji (f)	[lúgə tʃáji]
soup spoon	lugë gjelle (f)	[lúgə ɟéɫɛ]
fork	pirun (m)	[pirún]
knife	thikë (f)	[θíkə]

tableware (dishes)	enë kuzhine (f)	[énə kuʒínɛ]
plate (dinner ~)	pjatë (f)	[pjátə]
saucer	pjatë filxhani (f)	[pjátə fildʒáni]

shot glass	potir (m)	[potír]
glass (tumbler)	gotë (f)	[gótə]
cup	filxhan (m)	[fildʒán]

sugar bowl	tas për sheqer (m)	[tas pər ʃɛcér]
salt shaker	kripore (f)	[kripórɛ]
pepper shaker	enë piperi (f)	[énə pipéri]
butter dish	pjatë gjalpi (f)	[pjátə ɟálpi]

stock pot (soup pot)	tenxhere (f)	[tɛndʒérɛ]
frying pan (skillet)	tigan (m)	[tigán]
ladle	garuzhdë (f)	[garúʒdə]
colander	kullesë (f)	[kuɫésə]
tray (serving ~)	tabaka (f)	[tabaká]

bottle	shishe (f)	[ʃíʃɛ]
jar (glass)	kavanoz (m)	[kavanóz]
can	kanoçe (f)	[kanótʃɛ]

bottle opener	hapëse shishesh (f)	[hapəsé ʃíʃɛʃ]
can opener	hapëse kanoçesh (f)	[hapəsé kanótʃɛʃ]
corkscrew	turjelë tapash (f)	[turjélə tápaʃ]
filter	filtër (m)	[fíltər]
to filter (vt)	filtroj	[filtrój]

trash, garbage (food waste, etc.)	pleh (m)	[plɛh]
trash can (kitchen ~)	kosh plehrash (m)	[koʃ pléhraʃ]

72. Bathroom

bathroom	banjo (f)	[báɲo]
water	ujë (m)	[újə]
faucet	rubinet (m)	[rubinét]
hot water	ujë i nxehtë (f)	[újə i ndzéhtə]
cold water	ujë i ftohtë (f)	[újə i ftóhtə]

toothpaste	pastë dhëmbësh (f)	[pástə ðə́mbəʃ]
to brush one's teeth	laj dhëmbët	[laj ðə́mbət]

toothbrush	furçë dhëmbësh (f)	[fúrtʃə ðémbəʃ]
to shave (vi)	rruhem	[rúhɛm]
shaving foam	shkumë rroje (f)	[ʃkumə rójɛ]
razor	brisk (m)	[brísk]

to wash (one's hands, etc.)	laj duart	[laj dúart]
to take a bath	lahem	[láhɛm]
shower	dush (m)	[duʃ]
to take a shower	bëj dush	[bəj dúʃ]

bathtub	vaskë (f)	[váskə]
toilet (toilet bowl)	tualet (m)	[tualét]
sink (washbasin)	lavaman (m)	[lavamán]

| soap | sapun (m) | [sapún] |
| soap dish | pjatë sapuni (f) | [pjátə sapúni] |

sponge	sfungjer (m)	[sfunɟér]
shampoo	shampo (f)	[ʃampó]
towel	peshqir (m)	[pɛʃcír]
bathrobe	peshqir trupi (m)	[pɛʃcír trúpi]

laundry (laundering)	larje (f)	[lárjɛ]
washing machine	makinë larëse (f)	[makínə lárəsɛ]
to do the laundry	laj rroba	[laj róba]
laundry detergent	detergjent (m)	[dɛtɛrɟént]

73. Household appliances

TV set	televizor (m)	[tɛlɛvizór]
tape recorder	inçizues me shirit (m)	[intʃizúɛs mɛ ʃirít]
VCR (video recorder)	video regjistrues (m)	[vídɛo rɛɟistrúɛs]
radio	radio (f)	[rádio]
player (CD, MP3, etc.)	kasetofon (m)	[kasɛtofón]

video projector	projektor (m)	[projɛktór]
home movie theater	kinema shtëpie (f)	[kinɛmá ʃtəpíɛ]
DVD player	DVD player (m)	[dividí plɛjər]
amplifier	amplifikator (m)	[amplifikatór]
video game console	konsol video loje (m)	[konsól vídɛo lójɛ]

video camera	videokamerë (f)	[vidɛokamérə]
camera (photo)	aparat fotografik (m)	[aparát fotografík]
digital camera	kamerë digjitale (f)	[kamérə diɟitálɛ]

vacuum cleaner	fshesë elektrike (f)	[fʃésə ɛlɛktríkɛ]
iron (e.g., steam ~)	hekur (m)	[hékur]
ironing board	tryezë për hekurosje (f)	[tryézə pər hɛkurósjɛ]
telephone	telefon (m)	[tɛlɛfón]
cell phone	celular (m)	[tsɛlulár]

typewriter	**makinë shkrimi** (f)	[makínə ʃkrími]
sewing machine	**makinë qepëse** (f)	[makínə cépəsɛ]
microphone	**mikrofon** (m)	[mikrofón]
headphones	**kufje** (f)	[kúfjɛ]
remote control (TV)	**telekomandë** (f)	[tɛlɛkomándə]
CD, compact disc	**CD** (f)	[tsɛdé]
cassette, tape	**kasetë** (f)	[kasétə]
vinyl record	**pllakë gramafoni** (f)	[pɫákə gramafóni]

THE EARTH. WEATHER

T&P Books Publishing

space	**hapësirë** (f)	[hapəsírə]
space (as adj)	**hapësinor**	[hapəsinór]
outer space	**kozmos** (m)	[kozmós]
world	**botë** (f)	[bótə]
universe	**univers**	[univérs]
galaxy	**galaksi** (f)	[galaksí]
star	**yll** (m)	[yɫ]
constellation	**yllësi** (f)	[yɫəsí]
planet	**planet** (m)	[planét]
satellite	**satelit** (m)	[satɛlít]
meteorite	**meteor** (m)	[mɛtɛór]
comet	**kometë** (f)	[kométə]
asteroid	**asteroid** (m)	[astɛroíd]
orbit	**orbitë** (f)	[orbítə]
to revolve (~ around the Earth)	**rrotullohet**	[rotuɫóhɛt]
atmosphere	**atmosferë** (f)	[atmosférə]
the Sun	**Dielli** (m)	[diéɫi]
solar system	**sistemi diellor** (m)	[sistémi diɛɫór]
solar eclipse	**eklips diellor** (m)	[ɛklíps diɛɫór]
the Earth	**Toka** (f)	[tóka]
the Moon	**Hëna** (f)	[hə́na]
Mars	**Marsi** (m)	[mársi]
Venus	**Venera** (f)	[vɛnéra]
Jupiter	**Jupiteri** (m)	[jupitéri]
Saturn	**Saturni** (m)	[satúrni]
Mercury	**Merkuri** (m)	[mɛrkúri]
Uranus	**Urani** (m)	[uráni]
Neptune	**Neptuni** (m)	[nɛptúni]
Pluto	**Pluto** (f)	[plúto]
Milky Way	**Rruga e Qumështit** (f)	[rúga ɛ cúməʃtit]
Great Bear (Ursa Major)	**Arusha e Madhe** (f)	[arúʃa ɛ máðɛ]
North Star	**ylli i Veriut** (m)	[ýɫi i vériut]
Martian	**Marsian** (m)	[marsián]
extraterrestrial (n)	**jashtëtokësor** (m)	[jaʃtətokəsór]

alien	alien (m)	[alién]
flying saucer	disk fluturues (m)	[dísk fluturúɛs]
spaceship	anije kozmike (f)	[aníjɛ kozmíkɛ]
space station	stacion kozmik (m)	[statsión kozmík]
blast-off	ngritje (f)	[ŋrítjɛ]
engine	motor (m)	[motór]
nozzle	dizë (f)	[dízə]
fuel	karburant (m)	[karburánt]
cockpit, flight deck	kabinë pilotimi (f)	[kabínə pilotími]
antenna	antenë (f)	[anténə]
porthole	dritare anësore (f)	[dritárɛ anəsórɛ]
solar panel	panel solar (m)	[panél solár]
spacesuit	veshje astronauti (f)	[véʃjɛ astronáuti]
weightlessness	mungesë graviteti (f)	[muŋésə gravitéti]
oxygen	oksigjen (m)	[oksiɟén]
docking (in space)	ndërlidhje në hapësirë (f)	[ndərlíðjɛ nə hapəsírə]
to dock (vi, vt)	stacionohem	[statsionóhɛm]
observatory	observator (m)	[obsɛrvatór]
telescope	teleskop (m)	[tɛlɛskóp]
to observe (vt)	vëzhgoj	[vəʒgój]
to explore (vt)	eksploroj	[ɛksplorój]

75. The Earth

the Earth	Toka (f)	[tóka]
the globe (the Earth)	globi (f)	[glóbi]
planet	planet (m)	[planét]
atmosphere	atmosferë (f)	[atmosférə]
geography	gjeografi (f)	[ɟɛografí]
nature	natyrë (f)	[natýrə]
globe (table ~)	glob (m)	[glob]
map	hartë (f)	[hártə]
atlas	atlas (m)	[atlás]
Europe	Evropa (f)	[ɛvrópa]
Asia	Azia (f)	[azía]
Africa	Afrika (f)	[afríka]
Australia	Australia (f)	[australía]
America	Amerika (f)	[amɛríka]
North America	Amerika Veriore (f)	[amɛríka vɛriórɛ]
South America	Amerika Jugore (f)	[amɛríka jugórɛ]

| Antarctica | **Antarktika** (f) | [antarktíka] |
| the Arctic | **Arktiku** (m) | [arktíku] |

76. Cardinal directions

north	**veri** (m)	[vɛrí]
to the north	**drejt veriut**	[dréjt vériut]
in the north	**në veri**	[nə vɛrí]
northern (adj)	**verior**	[vɛriór]

south	**jug** (m)	[jug]
to the south	**drejt jugut**	[dréjt júgut]
in the south	**në jug**	[nə jug]
southern (adj)	**jugor**	[jugór]

west	**perëndim** (m)	[pɛrəndím]
to the west	**drejt perëndimit**	[dréjt pɛrəndímit]
in the west	**në perëndim**	[nə pɛrəndím]
western (adj)	**perëndimor**	[pɛrəndimór]

east	**lindje** (f)	[líndjɛ]
to the east	**drejt lindjes**	[dréjt líndjɛs]
in the east	**në lindje**	[nə líndjɛ]
eastern (adj)	**lindor**	[lindór]

77. Sea. Ocean

sea	**det** (m)	[dét]
ocean	**oqean** (m)	[ocɛán]
gulf (bay)	**gji** (m)	[ɟi]
straits	**ngushticë** (f)	[ŋuʃtítsə]

| land (solid ground) | **tokë** (f) | [tókə] |
| continent (mainland) | **kontinent** (m) | [kontinént] |

island	**ishull** (m)	[íʃuɫ]
peninsula	**gadishull** (m)	[gadíʃuɫ]
archipelago	**arkipelag** (m)	[arkipɛlág]

bay, cove	**gji** (m)	[ɟi]
harbor	**port** (m)	[port]
lagoon	**lagunë** (f)	[lagúnə]
cape	**kep** (m)	[kɛp]

atoll	**atol** (m)	[atól]
reef	**shkëmb nënujor** (m)	[ʃkəmb nənujór]
coral	**koral** (m)	[korál]
coral reef	**korale nënujorë** (f)	[korálɛ nənujórə]

deep (adj)	i thellë	[i θéɫə]
depth (deep water)	thellësi (f)	[θɛɫəsí]
abyss	humnerë (f)	[humnérə]
trench (e.g., Mariana ~)	hendek (m)	[hɛndék]

| current (Ocean ~) | rrymë (f) | [rýmə] |
| to surround (bathe) | rrethohet | [rɛθóhɛt] |

| shore | breg (m) | [brɛg] |
| coast | bregdet (m) | [brɛgdét] |

flow (flood tide)	batica (f)	[batítsa]
ebb (ebb tide)	zbaticë (f)	[zbatítsə]
shoal	cekëtinë (f)	[tsɛkətínə]
bottom (~ of the sea)	fund i detit (m)	[fúnd i détit]

wave	dallgë (f)	[dáɫgə]
crest (~ of a wave)	kreshtë (f)	[kréʃtə]
spume (sea foam)	shkumë (f)	[ʃkúmə]

storm (sea storm)	stuhi (f)	[stuhí]
hurricane	uragan (m)	[uragán]
tsunami	cunam (m)	[tsunám]
calm (dead ~)	qetësi (f)	[cɛtəsí]
quiet, calm (adj)	i qetë	[i cétə]

| pole | pol (m) | [pol] |
| polar (adj) | polar | [polár] |

latitude	gjerësi (f)	[ɟɛrəsí]
longitude	gjatësi (f)	[ɟatəsí]
parallel	paralele (f)	[paralélɛ]
equator	ekuator (m)	[ɛkuatór]

sky	qiell (m)	[cíɛɫ]
horizon	horizont (m)	[horizónt]
air	ajër (m)	[ájər]

lighthouse	fanar (m)	[fanár]
to dive (vi)	zhytem	[ʒýtɛm]
to sink (ab. boat)	fundosje	[fundósjɛ]
treasures	thesare (pl)	[θɛsárɛ]

78. Seas' and Oceans' names

Atlantic Ocean	Oqeani Atlantik (m)	[ocɛáni atlantík]
Indian Ocean	Oqeani Indian (m)	[ocɛáni indián]
Pacific Ocean	Oqeani Paqësor (m)	[ocɛáni pacəsór]
Arctic Ocean	Oqeani Arktik (m)	[ocɛáni arktík]
Black Sea	Deti i Zi (m)	[déti i zí]

Red Sea	Deti i Kuq (m)	[déti i kúc]
Yellow Sea	Deti i Verdhë (m)	[déti i vérðə]
White Sea	Deti i Bardhë (m)	[déti i bárðə]

Caspian Sea	Deti Kaspik (m)	[déti kaspík]
Dead Sea	Deti i Vdekur (m)	[déti i vdékur]
Mediterranean Sea	Deti Mesdhe (m)	[déti mɛsðé]

| Aegean Sea | Deti Egje (m) | [déti ɛɟé] |
| Adriatic Sea | Deti Adriatik (m) | [déti adriatík] |

Arabian Sea	Deti Arab (m)	[déti aráb]
Sea of Japan	Deti i Japonisë (m)	[déti i japonísə]
Bering Sea	Deti Bering (m)	[déti bériŋ]
South China Sea	Deti i Kinës Jugore (m)	[déti i kínəs jugórɛ]

Coral Sea	Deti Koral (m)	[déti korál]
Tasman Sea	Deti Tasman (m)	[déti tasmán]
Caribbean Sea	Deti i Karaibeve (m)	[déti i karaíbɛvɛ]

| Barents Sea | Deti Barents (m) | [déti barénts] |
| Kara Sea | Deti Kara (m) | [déti kára] |

North Sea	Deti i Veriut (m)	[déti i vériut]
Baltic Sea	Deti Baltik (m)	[déti baltík]
Norwegian Sea	Deti Norvegjez (m)	[déti norvɛɟéz]

79. Mountains

mountain	mal (m)	[mal]
mountain range	vargmal (m)	[vargmál]
mountain ridge	kresht malor (m)	[kréʃt malór]

summit, top	majë (f)	[májə]
peak	maja më e lartë (f)	[mája mə ɛ lártə]
foot (~ of the mountain)	rrëza e malit (f)	[rəza ɛ málit]
slope (mountainside)	shpat (m)	[ʃpat]

volcano	vullkan (m)	[vuɫkán]
active volcano	vullkan aktiv (m)	[vuɫkán aktív]
dormant volcano	vullkan i fjetur (m)	[vuɫkán i fjétur]

eruption	shpërthim (m)	[ʃpərθím]
crater	krater (m)	[kratér]
magma	magmë (f)	[mágmə]
lava	llavë (f)	[ɫávə]
molten (~ lava)	i shkrirë	[i ʃkrírə]

| canyon | kanion (m) | [kanión] |
| gorge | grykë (f) | [grýkə] |

| crevice | çarje (f) | [tʃárjɛ] |
| abyss (chasm) | humnerë (f) | [humnérə] |

pass, col	kalim (m)	[kalím]
plateau	pllajë (f)	[płájə]
cliff	shkëmb (m)	[ʃkəmb]
hill	kodër (f)	[kódər]

glacier	akullnajë (f)	[akułnájə]
waterfall	ujëvarë (f)	[ujəvárə]
geyser	gejzer (m)	[gɛjzér]
lake	liqen (m)	[licén]

plain	fushë (f)	[fúʃə]
landscape	peizazh (m)	[pɛizáʒ]
echo	jehonë (f)	[jɛhónə]

alpinist	alpinist (m)	[alpiníst]
rock climber	alpinist shkëmbßinjsh (m)	[alpiníst ʃkəmbiɲʃ]
to conquer (in climbing)	pushtoj majën	[puʃtój májən]
climb (an easy ~)	ngjitje (f)	[nɟítjɛ]

80. Mountains names

The Alps	Alpet (pl)	[alpét]
Mont Blanc	Montblanc (m)	[montblánk]
The Pyrenees	Pirenejet (pl)	[pirɛnéjɛt]

The Carpathians	Karpatet (m)	[karpátɛt]
The Ural Mountains	Malet Urale (pl)	[málɛt urálɛ]
The Caucasus Mountains	Malet Kaukaze (pl)	[málɛt kaukázɛ]
Mount Elbrus	Mali Elbrus (m)	[máli ɛlbrús]

The Altai Mountains	Malet Altai (pl)	[málɛt altái]
The Tian Shan	Tian Shani (m)	[tían ʃáni]
The Pamir Mountains	Malet e Pamirit (m)	[málɛt ɛ pamírit]
The Himalayas	Himalajet (pl)	[himalájɛt]
Mount Everest	Mali Everest (m)	[máli ɛvɛrést]

| The Andes | andet (pl) | [ándɛt] |
| Mount Kilimanjaro | Mali Kilimanxharo (m) | [máli kilimandʒáro] |

81. Rivers

river	lum (m)	[lum]
spring (natural source)	burim (m)	[burím]
riverbed (river channel)	shtrat lumi (m)	[ʃtrat lúmi]
basin (river valley)	basen (m)	[basén]

to flow into …	rrjedh …	[rjéð …]
tributary	derdhje (f)	[dérðjɛ]
bank (of river)	breg (m)	[brɛg]

current (stream)	rrymë (f)	[rýmə]
downstream (adv)	rrjedhje e poshtme	[rjéðjɛ ɛ póʃtmɛ]
upstream (adv)	rrjedhje e sipërme	[rjéðjɛ ɛ sípərmɛ]

inundation	vërshim (m)	[vərʃím]
flooding	përmbytje (f)	[pərmbýtjɛ]
to overflow (vi)	vërshon	[vərʃón]
to flood (vt)	përmbytet	[pərmbýtɛt]

| shallow (shoal) | cekëtinë (f) | [tsɛkətínə] |
| rapids | rrjedhë (f) | [rjéðə] |

dam	digë (f)	[dígə]
canal	kanal (m)	[kanál]
reservoir (artificial lake)	rezervuar (m)	[rɛzɛrvuár]
sluice, lock	pendë ujore (f)	[péndə ujórɛ]

water body (pond, etc.)	plan hidrik (m)	[plan hidrík]
swamp (marshland)	kënetë (f)	[kənétə]
bog, marsh	moçal (m)	[motʃ ál]
whirlpool	vorbull (f)	[vórbuɫ]

stream (brook)	përrua (f)	[pərúa]
drinking (ab. water)	i pijshëm	[i píjʃəm]
fresh (~ water)	i freskët	[i fréskət]

ice	akull (m)	[ákuɫ]
to freeze over	ngrihet	[ŋríhɛt]
(ab. river, etc.)		

82. Rivers' names

| Seine | Sena (f) | [séna] |
| Loire | Loire (f) | [luar] |

Thames	Temza (f)	[témza]
Rhine	Rajnë (m)	[rájnə]
Danube	Danubi (m)	[danúbi]

Volga	Volga (f)	[vólga]
Don	Doni (m)	[dóni]
Lena	Lena (f)	[léna]

Yellow River	Lumi i Verdhë (m)	[lúmi i vérðə]
Yangtze	Jangce (f)	[jaŋtsé]
Mekong	Mekong (m)	[mɛkóŋ]

Ganges	Gang (m)	[gaŋ]
Nile River	Lumi Nil (m)	[lúmi nil]
Congo River	Lumi Kongo (m)	[lúmi kóŋo]
Okavango River	Lumi Okavango (m)	[lúmi okaváŋo]
Zambezi River	Lumi Zambezi (m)	[lúmi zambézi]
Limpopo River	Lumi Limpopo (m)	[lúmi limpópo]
Mississippi River	Lumi Misisipi (m)	[lúmi misisípi]

83. Forest

| forest, wood | pyll (m) | [pyɬ] |
| forest (as adj) | pyjor | [pyjór] |

thick forest	pyll i ngjeshur (m)	[pyɬ i ɲjéʃur]
grove	zabel (m)	[zabél]
forest clearing	lëndinë (f)	[ləndínə]

| thicket | pyllëz (m) | [pýɬəz] |
| scrubland | shkurre (f) | [ʃkúrɛ] |

| footpath (troddenpath) | shteg (m) | [ʃtɛg] |
| gully | hon (m) | [hon] |

tree	pemë (f)	[pémə]
leaf	gjeth (m)	[ɟɛθ]
leaves (foliage)	gjethe (pl)	[ɟéθɛ]

fall of leaves	rënie e gjetheve (f)	[rəníɛ ɛ ɟéθɛvɛ]
to fall (ab. leaves)	bien	[bíɛn]
top (of the tree)	maje (f)	[májɛ]

branch	degë (f)	[dégə]
bough	degë (f)	[dégə]
bud (on shrub, tree)	syth (m)	[syθ]
needle (of pine tree)	shtiza pishe (f)	[ʃtíza píʃɛ]
pine cone	lule pishe (f)	[lúlɛ píʃɛ]

tree hollow	zgavër (f)	[zgávər]
nest	fole (f)	[folé]
burrow (animal hole)	strofull (f)	[strófuɬ]

trunk	trung (m)	[truŋ]
root	rrënjë (f)	[réɲə]
bark	lëvore (f)	[ləvórɛ]
moss	myshk (m)	[myʃk]

| to uproot (remove trees or tree stumps) | shkul | [ʃkul] |

| to chop down | pres | [prɛs] |
| to deforest (vt) | shpyllëzoj | [ʃpyɬəzój] |

tree stump	cung (m)	[tsún]
campfire	zjarr kampingu (m)	[zjar kampíŋu]
forest fire	zjarr në pyll (m)	[zjar nə pyɬ]
to extinguish (vt)	shuaj	[ʃúaj]

forest ranger	roje pyjore (f)	[rójɛ pyjórɛ]
protection	mbrojtje (f)	[mbrójtjɛ]
to protect (~ nature)	mbroj	[mbrój]
poacher	gjahtar i jashtëligjshëm (m)	[ɟahtár i jaʃtəliɟʃəm]
steel trap	grackë (f)	[grátskə]

| to gather, to pick (vt) | mbledh | [mbléð] |
| to lose one's way | humb rrugën | [húmb rúgən] |

84. Natural resources

natural resources	burime natyrore (pl)	[burímɛ natyrórɛ]
minerals	minerale (pl)	[minɛrálɛ]
deposits	depozita (pl)	[dɛpozíta]
field (e.g., oilfield)	fushë (f)	[fúʃə]

to mine (extract)	nxjerr	[ndzjér]
mining (extraction)	nxjerrje mineralesh (f)	[ndzjérjɛ minɛrálɛʃ]
ore	xehe (f)	[dzéhɛ]
mine (e.g., for coal)	minierë (f)	[miniérə]
shaft (mine ~)	nivel (m)	[nivél]
miner	minator (m)	[minatór]

| gas (natural ~) | gaz (m) | [gaz] |
| gas pipeline | gazsjellës (m) | [gazsjéɬəs] |

oil (petroleum)	naftë (f)	[náftə]
oil pipeline	naftësjellës (f)	[naftəsjéɬəs]
oil well	pus nafte (m)	[pus náftɛ]
derrick (tower)	burim nafte (m)	[burím náftɛ]
tanker	anije-cisternë (f)	[aníjɛ-tsistérnə]

sand	rërë (f)	[rərə]
limestone	gur gëlqeror (m)	[gur gəlcɛrór]
gravel	zhavorr (m)	[ʒavór]
peat	torfë (f)	[tórfə]
clay	argjilë (f)	[arɟílə]
coal	qymyr (m)	[cymýr]

iron (ore)	hekur (m)	[hékur]
gold	ar (m)	[ár]
silver	argjend (m)	[arɟénd]
nickel	nikel (m)	[nikél]
copper	bakër (m)	[bákər]

zinc	zink (m)	[zink]
manganese	mangan (m)	[maŋán]
mercury	merkur (m)	[mɛrkúr]
lead	plumb (m)	[plúmb]

mineral	mineral (m)	[minɛrál]
crystal	kristal (m)	[kristál]
marble	mermer (m)	[mɛrmér]
uranium	uranium (m)	[uraniúm]

85. Weather

weather	moti (m)	[móti]
weather forecast	parashikimi i motit (m)	[paraʃikími i mótit]
temperature	temperaturë (f)	[tɛmpɛratúrə]
thermometer	termometër (m)	[tɛrmométər]
barometer	barometër (m)	[barométər]

| humid (adj) | i lagësht | [i lágəʃt] |
| humidity | lagështi (f) | [lagəʃtí] |

heat (extreme ~)	vapë (f)	[vápə]
hot (torrid)	shumë nxehtë	[ʃúmə ndzéhtə]
it's hot	është nxehtë	[ə́ʃtə ndzéhtə]

| it's warm | është ngrohtë | [ə́ʃtə ŋróhtə] |
| warm (moderately hot) | ngrohtë | [ŋróhtə] |

| it's cold | bën ftohtë | [bən ftóhtə] |
| cold (adj) | i ftohtë | [i ftóhtə] |

sun	diell (m)	[díɛɫ]
to shine (vi)	ndriçon	[ndritʃón]
sunny (day)	me diell	[mɛ díɛɫ]
to come up (vi)	agon	[agón]
to set (vi)	perëndon	[pɛrəndón]

cloud	re (f)	[rɛ]
cloudy (adj)	vranët	[vránət]
rain cloud	re shiu (f)	[rɛ ʃíu]
somber (gloomy)	vranët	[vránət]

rain	shi (m)	[ʃi]
it's raining	bie shi	[bíɛ ʃi]
rainy (~ day, weather)	me shi	[mɛ ʃi]
to drizzle (vi)	shi i imët	[ʃi i ímət]

pouring rain	shi litar (m)	[ʃi litár]
downpour	stuhi shiu (f)	[stuhí ʃíu]
heavy (e.g., ~ rain)	i fortë	[i fórtə]

| puddle | brakë (f) | [brákə] |
| to get wet (in rain) | lagem | [lágɛm] |

fog (mist)	mjegull (f)	[mjéguɫ]
foggy	e mjegullt	[ɛ mjéguɫt]
snow	borë (f)	[bórə]
it's snowing	bie borë	[bíɛ bórə]

86. Severe weather. Natural disasters

thunderstorm	stuhi (f)	[stuhí]
lightning (~ strike)	vetëtimë (f)	[vɛtətímə]
to flash (vi)	vetëton	[vɛtətón]

thunder	bubullimë (f)	[bubuɫímə]
to thunder (vi)	bubullon	[bubuɫón]
it's thundering	bubullon	[bubuɫón]

| hail | breshër (m) | [bréʃər] |
| it's hailing | po bie breshër | [po biɛ bréʃər] |

| to flood (vt) | përmbytet | [pərmbýtɛt] |
| flood, inundation | përmbytje (f) | [pərmbýtjɛ] |

earthquake	tërmet (m)	[tərmét]
tremor, shoke	lëkundje (f)	[ləkúndjɛ]
epicenter	epiqendër (f)	[ɛpicéndər]

| eruption | shpërthim (m) | [ʃpərθím] |
| lava | llavë (f) | [ɫávə] |

twister	vorbull (f)	[vórbuɫ]
tornado	tornado (f)	[tornádo]
typhoon	tajfun (m)	[tajfún]

hurricane	uragan (m)	[uragán]
storm	stuhi (f)	[stuhí]
tsunami	cunam (m)	[tsunám]

cyclone	ciklon (m)	[tsiklón]
bad weather	mot i keq (m)	[mot i kɛc]
fire (accident)	zjarr (m)	[zjar]

| disaster | fatkeqësi (f) | [fatkɛcəsí] |
| meteorite | meteor (m) | [mɛtɛór] |

avalanche	ortek (m)	[orték]
snowslide	rrëshqitje bore (f)	[rəʃcítjɛ bórɛ]
blizzard	stuhi bore (f)	[stuhí bórɛ]
snowstorm	stuhi bore (f)	[stuhí bórɛ]

Tꭼp BOOKS

FAUNA

T&P Books Publishing

87. Mammals. Predators

predator	**grabitqar** (m)	[grabitcár]
tiger	**tigër** (m)	[tígər]
lion	**luan** (m)	[luán]
wolf	**ujk** (m)	[ujk]
fox	**dhelpër** (f)	[ðélpər]
jaguar	**jaguar** (m)	[jaguár]
leopard	**leopard** (m)	[lɛopárd]
cheetah	**gepard** (m)	[gɛpárd]
black panther	**panterë e zezë** (f)	[pantérə ɛ zézə]
puma	**puma** (f)	[púma]
snow leopard	**leopard i borës** (m)	[lɛopárd i bórəs]
lynx	**rrëqebull** (m)	[rəcébuɫ]
coyote	**kojotë** (f)	[kojótə]
jackal	**çakall** (m)	[tʃakáɫ]
hyena	**hienë** (f)	[hiénə]

88. Wild animals

animal	**kafshë** (f)	[káfʃə]
beast (animal)	**bishë** (f)	[bíʃə]
squirrel	**ketër** (m)	[kétər]
hedgehog	**iriq** (m)	[iríc]
hare	**lepur i egër** (m)	[lépur i égər]
rabbit	**lepur** (m)	[lépur]
badger	**vjedull** (f)	[vjéduɫ]
raccoon	**rakun** (m)	[rakún]
hamster	**hamster** (m)	[hamstér]
marmot	**marmot** (m)	[marmót]
mole	**urith** (m)	[uríθ]
mouse	**mi** (m)	[mi]
rat	**mi** (m)	[mi]
bat	**lakuriq** (m)	[lakuríc]
ermine	**herminë** (f)	[hɛrmínə]
sable	**kunadhe** (f)	[kunáðɛ]
marten	**shqarth** (m)	[ʃcarθ]

| weasel | nuselalë (f) | [nusɛlálə] |
| mink | vizon (m) | [vizón] |

| beaver | kastor (m) | [kastór] |
| otter | vidër (f) | [vídər] |

horse	kali (m)	[káli]
moose	dre brilopatë (m)	[drɛ brilopátə]
deer	dre (f)	[drɛ]
camel	deve (f)	[dévɛ]

bison	bizon (m)	[bizón]
wisent	bizon evropian (m)	[bizón ɛvropián]
buffalo	buall (m)	[búaɬ]

zebra	zebër (f)	[zébər]
antelope	antilopë (f)	[antilópə]
roe deer	dre (f)	[drɛ]
fallow deer	dre ugar (m)	[drɛ ugár]
chamois	kamosh (m)	[kamóʃ]
wild boar	derr i egër (m)	[dér i égər]

whale	balenë (f)	[balénə]
seal	fokë (f)	[fókə]
walrus	lopë deti (f)	[lópə déti]
fur seal	fokë (f)	[fókə]
dolphin	delfin (m)	[dɛlfín]

bear	ari (m)	[arí]
polar bear	ari polar (m)	[arí polár]
panda	panda (f)	[pánda]

monkey	majmun (m)	[majmún]
chimpanzee	shimpanze (f)	[ʃimpánzɛ]
orangutan	orangutan (m)	[oraŋután]
gorilla	gorillë (f)	[goríɬə]
macaque	majmun makao (m)	[majmún makáo]
gibbon	gibon (m)	[gibón]

| elephant | elefant (m) | [ɛlɛfánt] |
| rhinoceros | rinoqeront (m) | [rinocɛrónt] |

| giraffe | gjirafë (f) | [ɟiráfə] |
| hippopotamus | hipopotam (m) | [hipopotám] |

| kangaroo | kangur (m) | [kaŋúr] |
| koala (bear) | koala (f) | [koála] |

mongoose	mangustë (f)	[maŋústə]
chinchilla	çinçila (f)	[tʃintʃíla]
skunk	qelbës (m)	[célbəs]
porcupine	ferrëgjatë (m)	[fɛrəɟátə]

89. Domestic animals

cat	mace (f)	[mátsɛ]
tomcat	maçok (m)	[matʃók]
dog	qen (m)	[cɛn]

horse	kali (m)	[káli]
stallion (male horse)	hamshor (m)	[hamʃór]
mare	pelë (f)	[pélə]

cow	lopë (f)	[lópə]
bull	dem (m)	[dém]
ox	ka (m)	[ka]

sheep (ewe)	dele (f)	[délɛ]
ram	dash (m)	[daʃ]
goat	dhi (f)	[ðí]
billy goat, he-goat	cjap (m)	[tsjáp]

| donkey | gomar (m) | [gomár] |
| mule | mushkë (f) | [múʃkə] |

pig, hog	derr (m)	[dɛr]
piglet	derrkuc (m)	[dɛrkúts]
rabbit	lepur (m)	[lépur]

| hen (chicken) | pulë (f) | [púlə] |
| rooster | gjel (m) | [ɟél] |

duck	rosë (f)	[rósə]
drake	rosak (m)	[rosák]
goose	patë (f)	[pátə]

| tom turkey, gobbler | gjel deti i egër (m) | [ɟél déti i égər] |
| turkey (hen) | gjel deti (m) | [ɟél déti] |

domestic animals	kafshë shtëpiake (f)	[káfʃə ʃtəpiákɛ]
tame (e.g., ~ hamster)	i zbutur	[i zbútur]
to tame (vt)	zbus	[zbus]
to breed (vt)	rrit	[rit]

farm	fermë (f)	[férmə]
poultry	pulari (f)	[pularí]
cattle	bagëti (f)	[bagətí]
herd (cattle)	kope (f)	[kopé]

stable	stallë (f)	[stáłə]
pigpen	stallë e derrave (f)	[stáłə ɛ déravɛ]
cowshed	stallë e lopëve (f)	[stáłə ɛ lópəvɛ]
rabbit hutch	kolibe lepujsh (f)	[kolíbɛ lépujʃ]
hen house	kotec (m)	[kotéts]

90. Birds

bird	zog (m)	[zog]
pigeon	pëllumb (m)	[pełúmb]
sparrow	harabel (m)	[harabél]
tit (great tit)	xhixhimës (m)	[dʒidʒimés]
magpie	laraskë (f)	[laráskə]

raven	korb (m)	[korb]
crow	sorrë (f)	[sórə]
jackdaw	galë (f)	[gálə]
rook	sorrë (f)	[sórə]

duck	rosë (f)	[rósə]
goose	patë (f)	[pátə]
pheasant	fazan (m)	[fazán]

eagle	shqiponjë (f)	[ʃcipóɲə]
hawk	gjeraqinë (f)	[ɟɛracínə]
falcon	fajkua (f)	[fajkúa]
vulture	hutë (f)	[hútə]
condor (Andean ~)	kondor (m)	[kondór]

swan	mjellmë (f)	[mjéłmə]
crane	lejlek (m)	[lɛjlék]
stork	lejlek (m)	[lɛjlék]

parrot	papagall (m)	[papagáł]
hummingbird	kolibri (m)	[kolíbri]
peacock	pallua (m)	[pałúa]

ostrich	struc (m)	[struts]
heron	çafkë (f)	[tʃáfkə]
flamingo	flamingo (m)	[flamíŋo]
pelican	pelikan (m)	[pɛlikán]

nightingale	bilbil (m)	[bilbíl]
swallow	dallëndyshe (f)	[dałəndýʃɛ]

thrush	mëllenjë (f)	[mətéɲə]
song thrush	grifsha (f)	[grífʃa]
blackbird	mëllenjë (f)	[mətéɲə]

swift	dallëndyshe (f)	[dałəndýʃɛ]
lark	thëllëzë (f)	[θətézə]
quail	trumcak (m)	[trumtsák]

woodpecker	qukapik (m)	[cukapík]
cuckoo	kukuvajkë (f)	[kukuvájkə]
owl	buf (m)	[buf]
eagle owl	buf mbretëror (m)	[buf mbrɛtərór]

wood grouse	**fazan i pyllit** (m)	[fazán i pýłit]
black grouse	**fazan i zi** (m)	[fazán i zí]
partridge	**thëllëzë** (f)	[θəłéezə]

starling	**gargull** (m)	[gárguł]
canary	**kanarinë** (f)	[kanarínə]
hazel grouse	**fazan mali** (m)	[fazán máli]
chaffinch	**trishtil** (m)	[triʃtíl]
bullfinch	**trishtil dimri** (m)	[triʃtíl dímri]

seagull	**pulëbardhë** (f)	[puləbárðə]
albatross	**albatros** (m)	[albatrós]
penguin	**penguin** (m)	[pɛŋuín]

91. Fish. Marine animals

bream	**krapuliq** (m)	[krapulíc]
carp	**krap** (m)	[krap]
perch	**perç** (m)	[pɛrtʃ]
catfish	**mustak** (m)	[musták]
pike	**mlysh** (m)	[mlýʃ]

salmon	**salmon** (m)	[salmón]
sturgeon	**bli** (m)	[blí]

herring	**harengë** (f)	[haréŋə]
Atlantic salmon	**salmon Atlantiku** (m)	[salmón atlantíku]
mackerel	**skumbri** (m)	[skúmbri]
flatfish	**shojzë** (f)	[ʃójzə]

zander, pike perch	**troftë** (f)	[tróftə]
cod	**merluc** (m)	[mɛrlúts]
tuna	**tunë** (f)	[túnə]
trout	**troftë** (f)	[tróftə]

eel	**ngjalë** (f)	[nɟálə]
electric ray	**peshk elektrik** (m)	[pɛʃk ɛlɛktrík]
moray eel	**ngjalë morel** (f)	[nɟálə morél]
piranha	**piranja** (f)	[piráɲa]

shark	**peshkaqen** (m)	[pɛʃkacén]
dolphin	**delfin** (m)	[dɛlfín]
whale	**balenë** (f)	[balénə]

crab	**gaforre** (f)	[gafórɛ]
jellyfish	**kandil deti** (m)	[kandíl déti]
octopus	**oktapod** (m)	[oktapód]

starfish	**yll deti** (m)	[yɬ déti]
sea urchin	**iriq deti** (m)	[iríc déti]

seahorse	kalë deti (m)	[kálə déti]
oyster	midhje (f)	[míðjɛ]
shrimp	karkalec (m)	[karkaléts]
lobster	karavidhe (f)	[karavíðɛ]
spiny lobster	karavidhe (f)	[karavíðɛ]

92. Amphibians. Reptiles

snake	gjarpër (m)	[ɟárpər]
venomous (snake)	helmues	[hɛlmúɛs]
viper	nepërka (f)	[nɛpérka]
cobra	kobra (f)	[kóbra]
python	piton (m)	[pitón]
boa	boa (f)	[bóa]
grass snake	kular (m)	[kulár]
rattle snake	gjarpër me zile (m)	[ɟárpər mɛ zílɛ]
anaconda	anakonda (f)	[anakónda]
lizard	hardhucë (f)	[harðútsə]
iguana	iguana (f)	[iguána]
monitor lizard	varan (m)	[varán]
salamander	salamandër (f)	[salamándər]
chameleon	kameleon (m)	[kamɛlɛón]
scorpion	akrep (m)	[akrép]
turtle	breshkë (f)	[bréʃkə]
frog	bretkosë (f)	[brɛtkósə]
toad	zhabë (f)	[ʒábə]
crocodile	krokodil (m)	[krokodíl]

93. Insects

insect, bug	insekt (m)	[insékt]
butterfly	flutur (f)	[flútur]
ant	milingonë (f)	[miliŋónə]
fly	mizë (f)	[mízə]
mosquito	mushkonjë (f)	[muʃkóɲə]
beetle	brumbull (m)	[brúmbuɫ]
wasp	grerëz (f)	[grérəz]
bee	bletë (f)	[blétə]
bumblebee	greth (m)	[grɛθ]
gadfly (botfly)	zekth (m)	[zɛkθ]
spider	merimangë (f)	[mɛrimáŋə]
spiderweb	rrjetë merimange (f)	[rjétə mɛrimáɲɛ]

dragonfly	**pilivesë** (f)	[pilivésə]
grasshopper	**karkalec** (m)	[karkaléts]
moth (night butterfly)	**molë** (f)	[mólə]

cockroach	**kacabu** (f)	[katsabú]
tick	**rriqër** (m)	[rícər]
flea	**plesht** (m)	[plɛʃt]
midge	**mushicë** (f)	[muʃítsə]

locust	**gjinkallë** (f)	[ɟinkáɫə]
snail	**kërmill** (m)	[kərmíɫ]
cricket	**bulkth** (m)	[búlkθ]
lightning bug	**xixëllonjë** (f)	[dzidzəɫóɲə]
ladybug	**mollëkuqe** (f)	[moɫəkúcɛ]
cockchafer	**vizhë** (f)	[víʒə]

leech	**shushunjë** (f)	[ʃuʃúɲə]
caterpillar	**vemje** (f)	[vémjɛ]
earthworm	**krimb toke** (m)	[krímb tókɛ]
larva	**larvë** (f)	[lárvə]

FLORA

T&P Books Publishing

tree	pemë (f)	[pémə]
deciduous (adj)	gjethor	[ɟɛθór]
coniferous (adj)	halor	[halór]
evergreen (adj)	përherë të gjelbra	[pərhérə tə ɟélbra]

apple tree	pemë molle (f)	[pémə mótɛ]
pear tree	pemë dardhe (f)	[pémə dárðɛ]
sweet cherry tree	pemë qershie (f)	[pémə cɛrʃíɛ]
sour cherry tree	pemë qershi vishnje (f)	[pémə cɛrʃí víʃɲɛ]
plum tree	pemë kumbulle (f)	[pémə kúmbuɫɛ]

birch	mështekna (f)	[məʃtékna]
oak	lis (m)	[lis]
linden tree	bli (m)	[blí]
aspen	plep i egër (m)	[plɛp i égər]
maple	panjë (f)	[páɲə]

spruce	bredh (m)	[brɛð]
pine	pishë (f)	[píʃə]
larch	larsh (m)	[lárʃ]

| fir tree | bredh i bardhë (m) | [brɛð i bárðə] |
| cedar | kedër (m) | [kédər] |

| poplar | plep (m) | [plɛp] |
| rowan | vadhë (f) | [váðə] |

| willow | shelg (m) | [ʃɛlg] |
| alder | verr (m) | [vɛr] |

| beech | ah (m) | [ah] |
| elm | elm (m) | [élm] |

| ash (tree) | shelg (m) | [ʃɛlg] |
| chestnut | gështenjë (f) | [gəʃtéɲə] |

magnolia	manjolia (f)	[maɲólia]
palm tree	palma (f)	[pálma]
cypress	qiparis (m)	[ciparís]

mangrove	rizoforë (f)	[rizofórə]
baobab	baobab (m)	[baobáb]
eucalyptus	eukalipt (m)	[ɛukalípt]
sequoia	sekuojë (f)	[sɛkuójə]

95. Shrubs

| bush | shkurre (f) | [ʃkúrɛ] |
| shrub | kaçube (f) | [katʃúbɛ] |

| grapevine | hardhi (f) | [harðí] |
| vineyard | vreshtë (f) | [vréʃtə] |

raspberry bush	mjedër (f)	[mjédər]
blackcurrant bush	kaliboba e zezë (f)	[kalibóba ɛ zézə]
redcurrant bush	kaliboba e kuqe (f)	[kalibóba ɛ kúcɛ]
gooseberry bush	shkurre kulumbrie (f)	[ʃkúrɛ kulumbríɛ]

acacia	akacie (f)	[akátsiɛ]
barberry	krespinë (f)	[krɛspínə]
jasmine	jasemin (m)	[jasɛmín]

juniper	dëllinjë (f)	[dəłíɲə]
rosebush	trëndafil (m)	[trəndafíl]
dog rose	trëndafil i egër (m)	[trəndafíl i égər]

96. Fruits. Berries

| fruit | frut (m) | [frut] |
| fruits | fruta (pl) | [frúta] |

apple	mollë (f)	[mółə]
pear	dardhë (f)	[dárðə]
plum	kumbull (f)	[kúmbuł]

strawberry (garden ~)	luleshtrydhe (f)	[lulɛʃtrýðɛ]
sour cherry	qershi vishnje (f)	[cɛrʃí víʃɲɛ]
sweet cherry	qershi (f)	[cɛrʃí]
grape	rrush (m)	[ruʃ]

raspberry	mjedër (f)	[mjédər]
blackcurrant	kaliboba e zezë (f)	[kalibóba ɛ zézə]
redcurrant	kaliboba e kuqe (f)	[kalibóba ɛ kúcɛ]
gooseberry	kulumbri (f)	[kulumbrí]
cranberry	boronica (f)	[boronítsa]

orange	portokall (m)	[portokáł]
mandarin	mandarinë (f)	[mandarínə]
pineapple	ananas (m)	[ananás]
banana	banane (f)	[banánɛ]
date	hurmë (f)	[húrmə]

| lemon | limon (m) | [limón] |
| apricot | kajsi (f) | [kajsí] |

peach	pjeshkë (f)	[pjéʃkə]
kiwi	kivi (m)	[kívi]
grapefruit	grejpfrut (m)	[grɛjpfrút]

berry	manë (f)	[mánə]
berries	mana (f)	[mána]
cowberry	boronicë mirtile (f)	[boronítsə mirtílɛ]
wild strawberry	luleshtrydhe e egër (f)	[lulɛʃtrýðɛ ɛ égər]
bilberry	boronicë (f)	[boronítsə]

97. Flowers. Plants

| flower | lule (f) | [lúlɛ] |
| bouquet (of flowers) | buqetë (f) | [bucétə] |

rose (flower)	trëndafil (m)	[trəndafíl]
tulip	tulipan (m)	[tulipán]
carnation	karafil (m)	[karafíl]
gladiolus	gladiolë (f)	[gladiólə]

cornflower	lule misri (f)	[lúlɛ mísri]
harebell	lule këmborë (f)	[lúlɛ kəmbórə]
dandelion	luleradhiqe (f)	[lulɛraðícɛ]
camomile	kamomil (m)	[kamomíl]

aloe	aloe (f)	[alóɛ]
cactus	kaktus (m)	[kaktús]
rubber plant, ficus	fikus (m)	[fíkus]

lily	zambak (m)	[zambák]
geranium	barbarozë (f)	[barbarózə]
hyacinth	zymbyl (m)	[zymbýl]

mimosa	mimoza (f)	[mimóza]
narcissus	narcis (m)	[nartsís]
nasturtium	lule këmbore (f)	[lúlɛ kəmbórɛ]

orchid	orkide (f)	[orkidé]
peony	bozhure (f)	[boʒúrɛ]
violet	vjollcë (f)	[vjółtsə]

pansy	lule vjollca (f)	[lúlɛ vjółtsa]
forget-me-not	mosmëharro (f)	[mosməharó]
daisy	margaritë (f)	[margarítə]

poppy	lulëkuqe (f)	[luləkúcɛ]
hemp	kërp (m)	[kérp]
mint	mendër (f)	[méndər]
lily of the valley	zambak i fushës (m)	[zambák i fúʃəs]
snowdrop	luleborë (f)	[lulɛbórə]

nettle	hithra (f)	[híθra]
sorrel	lëpjeta (f)	[ləpjéta]
water lily	zambak uji (m)	[zambák úji]
fern	fier (m)	[fíɛr]
lichen	likene (f)	[likénɛ]

conservatory (greenhouse)	serrë (f)	[sérə]
lawn	lëndinë (f)	[ləndínə]
flowerbed	kënd lulishteje (m)	[kənd lulíʃtɛjɛ]

plant	bimë (f)	[bímə]
grass	bar (m)	[bar]
blade of grass	fije bari (f)	[fíjɛ bári]

leaf	gjeth (m)	[ɟɛθ]
petal	petale (f)	[pɛtálɛ]
stem	bisht (m)	[biʃt]
tuber	zhardhok (m)	[ʒarðók]

| young plant (shoot) | filiz (m) | [filíz] |
| thorn | gjemb (m) | [ɟémb] |

to blossom (vi)	lulëzoj	[luləzój]
to fade, to wither	vyshket	[výʃkɛt]
smell (odor)	aromë (f)	[arómə]
to cut (flowers)	pres lulet	[prɛs lúlɛt]
to pick (a flower)	mbledh lule	[mbléð lúlɛ]

98. Cereals, grains

grain	drithë (m)	[dríθə]
cereal crops	drithëra (pl)	[dríθəra]
ear (of barley, etc.)	kaush (m)	[kaúʃ]

wheat	grurë (f)	[grúrə]
rye	thekër (f)	[θékər]
oats	tërshërë (f)	[tərʃérə]

| millet | mel (m) | [mɛl] |
| barley | elb (m) | [ɛlb] |

corn	misër (m)	[mísər]
rice	oriz (m)	[oríz]
buckwheat	hikërr (m)	[híkər]

pea plant	bizele (f)	[bizélɛ]
kidney bean	groshë (f)	[gróʃə]
soy	sojë (f)	[sójə]
lentil	thjerrëz (f)	[θjérəz]
beans (pulse crops)	fasule (f)	[fasúlɛ]

T&P BOOKS

COUNTRIES OF
THE WORLD

T&P Books Publishing

Afghanistan	**Afganistan** (m)	[afganistán]
Albania	**Shqipëri** (f)	[ʃcipərí]
Argentina	**Argjentinë** (f)	[arɲɛntínə]
Armenia	**Armeni** (f)	[armɛní]
Australia	**Australia** (f)	[australía]
Austria	**Austri** (f)	[austrí]
Azerbaijan	**Azerbajxhan** (m)	[azɛrbajdʒán]

The Bahamas	**Bahamas** (m)	[bahámas]
Bangladesh	**Bangladesh** (m)	[baŋladéʃ]
Belarus	**Bjellorusi** (f)	[bjɛɫorusí]
Belgium	**Belgjikë** (f)	[bɛʎíkə]
Bolivia	**Bolivi** (f)	[bolliví]
Bosnia and Herzegovina	**Bosnje Herzegovina** (f)	[bósɲɛ hɛrzɛgovína]
Brazil	**Brazil** (m)	[brazíl]
Bulgaria	**Bullgari** (f)	[buɫgarí]

Cambodia	**Kamboxhia** (f)	[kambódʒia]
Canada	**Kanada** (f)	[kanadá]
Chile	**Kili** (m)	[kíli]
China	**Kinë** (f)	[kínə]
Colombia	**Kolumbi** (f)	[kolumbí]
Croatia	**Kroaci** (f)	[kroatsí]
Cuba	**Kuba** (f)	[kúba]
Cyprus	**Qipro** (f)	[cípro]
Czech Republic	**Republika Çeke** (f)	[rɛpublíka tʃékɛ]

Denmark	**Danimarkë** (f)	[danimárkə]
Dominican Republic	**Republika Dominikane** (f)	[rɛpublíka dominikánɛ]
Ecuador	**Ekuador** (m)	[ɛkuadór]
Egypt	**Egjipt** (m)	[ɛɟípt]
England	**Angli** (f)	[aŋlí]
Estonia	**Estoni** (f)	[ɛstoní]
Finland	**Finlandë** (f)	[finlándə]
France	**Francë** (f)	[frántsə]
French Polynesia	**Polinezia Franceze** (f)	[polinɛzía frantsézɛ]

Georgia	**Gjeorgji** (f)	[ɟeoɟí]
Germany	**Gjermani** (f)	[ɟɛrmaní]
Ghana	**Gana** (f)	[gána]
Great Britain	**Britani e Madhe** (f)	[brítani ɛ máðɛ]
Greece	**Greqi** (f)	[grɛcí]
Haiti	**Haiti** (m)	[haíti]
Hungary	**Hungari** (f)	[huŋarí]

100. Countries. Part 2

Iceland	Islandë (f)	[islándə]
India	Indi (f)	[indí]
Indonesia	Indonezi (f)	[indonɛzí]
Iran	Iran (m)	[irán]
Iraq	Irak (m)	[irak]
Ireland	Irlandë (f)	[irlándə]
Israel	Izrael (m)	[izraél]
Italy	Itali (f)	[italí]

Jamaica	Xhamajka (f)	[dʒamájka]
Japan	Japoni (f)	[japoní]
Jordan	Jordani (f)	[jordaní]
Kazakhstan	Kazakistan (m)	[kazakistán]
Kenya	Kenia (f)	[kénia]
Kirghizia	Kirgistan (m)	[kirgistán]
Kuwait	Kuvajt (m)	[kuvájt]

Laos	Laos (m)	[láos]
Latvia	Letoni (f)	[lɛtoní]
Lebanon	Liban (m)	[libán]
Libya	Libia (f)	[libía]
Liechtenstein	Lichtenstein (m)	[litshtɛnstéin]
Lithuania	Lituani (f)	[lituaní]
Luxembourg	Luksemburg (m)	[luksɛmbúrg]
Macedonia (Republic of ~)	Maqedonia (f)	[macɛdonía]
Madagascar	Madagaskar (m)	[madagaskár]
Malaysia	Malajzi (f)	[malajzí]
Malta	Maltë (f)	[máltə]
Mexico	Meksikë (f)	[mɛksíkə]
Moldova, Moldavia	Moldavi (f)	[moldaví]
Monaco	Monako (f)	[monáko]
Mongolia	Mongoli (f)	[moŋolí]
Montenegro	Mali i Zi (m)	[máli i zí]
Morocco	Marok (m)	[marók]
Myanmar	Mianmar (m)	[mianmár]

Namibia	Namibia (f)	[namíbia]
Nepal	Nepal (m)	[nɛpál]
Netherlands	Holandë (f)	[holándə]
New Zealand	Zelandë e Re (f)	[zɛlándə ɛ ré]
North Korea	Korea e Veriut (f)	[koréa ɛ vériut]
Norway	Norvegji (f)	[norvɛɟí]

101. Countries. Part 3

Pakistan	Pakistan (m)	[pakistán]
Palestine	Palestinë (f)	[palɛstínə]

Panama	Panama (f)	[panamá]
Paraguay	Paraguai (m)	[paraguái]
Peru	Peru (f)	[pɛrú]
Poland	Poloni (f)	[poloní]
Portugal	Portugali (f)	[portugalí]
Romania	Rumani (f)	[rumaní]
Russia	Rusi (f)	[rusí]

Saudi Arabia	Arabia Saudite (f)	[arabía saudítɛ]
Scotland	Skoci (f)	[skotsí]
Senegal	Senegal (m)	[sɛnɛgál]
Serbia	Serbi (f)	[sɛrbí]
Slovakia	Sllovaki (f)	[słovakí]
Slovenia	Sllovenia (f)	[słovɛnía]

South Africa	Afrika e Jugut (f)	[afríka ɛ júgut]
South Korea	Korea e Jugut (f)	[koréa ɛ júgut]
Spain	Spanjë (f)	[spáɲə]
Suriname	Surinam (m)	[surinám]
Sweden	Suedi (f)	[suɛdí]
Switzerland	Zvicër (f)	[zvítsər]
Syria	Siri (f)	[sirí]

Taiwan	Tajvan (m)	[tajván]
Tajikistan	Taxhikistan (m)	[tadʒikistán]
Tanzania	Tanzani (f)	[tanzaní]
Tasmania	Tasmani (f)	[tasmaní]
Thailand	Tajlandë (f)	[tajlándə]
Tunisia	Tunizi (f)	[tunizí]
Turkey	Turqi (f)	[turcí]
Turkmenistan	Turkmenistan (m)	[turkmɛnistán]

Ukraine	Ukrainë (f)	[ukraínə]
United Arab Emirates	Emiratet e Bashkuara Arabe (pl)	[ɛmirátɛt ɛ baʃkúara arábɛ]
United States of America	Shtetet e Bashkuara të Amerikës	[ʃtétɛt ɛ baʃkúara tə amɛríkəs]
Uruguay	Uruguai (m)	[uruguái]
Uzbekistan	Uzbekistan (m)	[uzbɛkistán]

Vatican	Vatikan (m)	[vatikán]
Venezuela	Venezuelë (f)	[vɛnɛzuélə]
Vietnam	Vietnam (m)	[viɛtnám]
Zanzibar	Zanzibar (m)	[zanzibár]

GASTRONOMIC GLOSSARY

This section contains a lot of words and terms associated with food. This dictionary will make it easier for you to understand the menu at a restaurant and choose the right dish

T&P Books Publishing

aftertaste	shije (f)	[ʃíjɛ]
almond	bajame (f)	[bajámɛ]
anise	anisetë (f)	[anisétə]
aperitif	aperitiv (m)	[apɛritív]
appetite	oreks (m)	[oréks]
appetizer	antipastë (f)	[antipástə]
apple	mollë (f)	[móɬə]
apricot	kajsi (f)	[kajsí]
artichoke	angjinare (f)	[anɟinárɛ]
asparagus	asparagus (m)	[asparágus]
Atlantic salmon	salmon Atlantiku (m)	[salmón atlantíku]
avocado	avokado (f)	[avokádo]
bacon	proshutë (f)	[proʃútə]
banana	banane (f)	[banánɛ]
barley	elb (m)	[ɛlb]
bartender	banakier (m)	[banakiér]
basil	borzilok (m)	[borzilók]
bay leaf	gjeth dafine (m)	[ɟɛθ dafínɛ]
beans	fasule (f)	[fasúlɛ]
beef	mish lope (m)	[miʃ lópɛ]
beer	birrë (f)	[bírə]
beet	panxhar (m)	[pandʒár]
bell pepper	spec (m)	[spɛts]
berries	mana (f)	[mána]
berry	manë (f)	[mánə]
bilberry	boronicë (f)	[boronítsə]
birch bolete	porcinela (f)	[portsinéla]
bitter	i hidhur	[i hiður]
black coffee	kafe e zezë (f)	[káfɛ ɛ zézə]
black pepper	piper i zi (m)	[pipér i zi]
black tea	çaj i zi (m)	[tʃáj i zí]
blackberry	manaferra (f)	[manaféra]
blackcurrant	kaliboba e zezë (f)	[kalibóba ɛ zézə]
boiled	i zier	[i zíɛr]
bottle opener	hapëse shishesh (f)	[hapəsɛ ʃíʃɛʃ]
bread	bukë (f)	[búkə]
breakfast	mëngjes (m)	[mənɟés]
bream	krapuliq (m)	[krapulíc]
broccoli	brokoli (m)	[brókoli]
Brussels sprouts	lakër Brukseli (f)	[lákər brukséli]
buckwheat	hikërr (m)	[híkər]
butter	gjalp (m)	[ɟalp]
buttercream	krem gjalpi (m)	[krɛm ɟálpi]
cabbage	lakër (f)	[lákər]

cake	kek (m)	[kék]
cake	tortë (f)	[tórtə]
calorie	kalori (f)	[kalorí]
can opener	hapëse kanoçesh (f)	[hapəsé kanótʃɛʃ]
candy	karamele (f)	[karamélɛ]
canned food	konserva (f)	[konsérva]
cappuccino	kapuçino (m)	[kaputʃíno]
caraway	kumin (m)	[kumín]
carbohydrates	karbohidrat (m)	[karbohidrát]
carbonated	ujë i karbonuar	[újə i karbonúar]
carp	krap (m)	[krap]
carrot	karotë (f)	[karótə]
catfish	mustak (m)	[musták]
cauliflower	lulelakër (f)	[lulɛlákər]
caviar	havjar (m)	[havjár]
celery	selino (f)	[sɛlíno]
cep	porcini (m)	[portsíni]
cereal crops	drithëra (pl)	[dríθəra]
champagne	shampanjë (f)	[ʃampáɲə]
chanterelle	shanterele (f)	[ʃantɛrélɛ]
check	faturë (f)	[fatúrə]
cheese	djath (m)	[djáθ]
chewing gum	çamçakëz (m)	[tʃamtʃakéz]
chicken	pulë (f)	[púlə]
chocolate	çokollatë (f)	[tʃokołátə]
chocolate	prej çokollate	[prɛj tʃokołátɛ]
cinnamon	kanellë (f)	[kanéłə]
clear soup	lëng mishi (m)	[ləŋ míʃi]
cloves	karafil (m)	[karafíl]
cocktail	koktej (m)	[koktéj]
coconut	arrë kokosi (f)	[árə kokósi]
cod	merluc (m)	[mɛrlúts]
coffee	kafe (f)	[káfɛ]
coffee with milk	kafe me qumësht (m)	[káfɛ mɛ cúməʃt]
cognac	konjak (m)	[koɲák]
cold	i ftohtë	[i ftóhtə]
condensed milk	qumësht i kondensuar (m)	[cúməʃt i kondɛnsúar]
condiment	salcë (f)	[sáltsə]
confectionery	ëmbëlsira (pl)	[əmbəlsíra]
cookies	biskota (pl)	[biskóta]
coriander	koriandër (m)	[koriándər]
corkscrew	turjelë tapash (f)	[turjélə tápaʃ]
corn	misër (m)	[mísər]
corn	misër (m)	[mísər]
cornflakes	kornfleiks (m)	[kornfléiks]
course, dish	pjatë (f)	[pjátə]
cowberry	boronicë mirtile (f)	[boronítsə mirtílɛ]
crab	gaforre (f)	[gafórɛ]
cranberry	boronica (f)	[boronítsa]
cream	krem qumështi (m)	[krɛm cúməʃti]
crumb	dromcë (f)	[drómtsə]
crustaceans	krustace (pl)	[krustátsɛ]

cucumber	kastravec (m)	[kastravéts]
cuisine	kuzhinë (f)	[kuʒínə]
cup	filxhan (m)	[fildʒán]
dark beer	birrë e zezë (f)	[bírə ɛ zézə]
date	hurmë (f)	[húrmə]
death cap	kërpudha e vdekjes (f)	[kərpúða ɛ vdékjɛs]
dessert	ëmbëlsirë (f)	[əmbəlsírə]
diet	dietë (f)	[diétə]
dill	kopër (f)	[kópər]
dinner	darkë (f)	[dárkə]
dried	i tharë	[i θárə]
drinking water	ujë i pijshëm (m)	[újə i píjʃəm]
duck	rosë (f)	[rósə]
ear	kaush (m)	[kaúʃ]
edible mushroom	kërpudhë ushqyese (f)	[kərpúðə uʃcýɛsɛ]
eel	ngjalë (f)	[ɲálə]
egg	ve (f)	[vɛ]
egg white	e bardhë veze (f)	[ɛ bárðə vézɛ]
egg yolk	e verdhë veze (f)	[ɛ vérðə vézɛ]
eggplant	patëllxhan (m)	[patəłdʒán]
eggs	vezë (pl)	[vézə]
Enjoy your meal!	Të bëftë mirë!	[tə bəftə mírə!]
fats	yndyrë (f)	[yndýrə]
fig	fik (m)	[fik]
filling	mbushje (f)	[mbúʃjɛ]
fish	peshk (m)	[pɛʃk]
flatfish	shojzë (f)	[ʃójzə]
flour	miell (m)	[míɛł]
fly agaric	kësulkuqe (f)	[kəsulkúcɛ]
food	ushqim (m)	[uʃcím]
fork	pirun (m)	[pirún]
freshly squeezed juice	lëng frutash i freskët (m)	[lən frútaʃ i fréskət]
fried	i skuqur	[i skúcur]
fried eggs	vezë të skuqura (pl)	[vézə tə skúcura]
frozen	i ngrirë	[i ŋrírə]
fruit	frut (m)	[frut]
fruits	fruta (pl)	[frúta]
game	gjah (m)	[ɉáh]
gammon	kofshë derri (f)	[kófʃə déri]
garlic	hudhër (f)	[húðər]
gin	xhin (m)	[dʒin]
ginger	xhenxhefil (m)	[dʒɛndʒɛfíl]
glass	gotë (f)	[gótə]
glass	gotë vere (f)	[gótə vérɛ]
goose	patë (f)	[pátə]
gooseberry	kulumbri (f)	[kulumbrí]
grain	drithë (m)	[dríθə]
grape	rrush (m)	[ruʃ]
grapefruit	grejpfrut (m)	[grɛjpfrút]
green tea	çaj jeshil (m)	[tʃáj jɛʃíl]
greens	zarzavate (pl)	[zarzavátɛ]
groats	drithëra (pl)	[dríθəra]

halibut	shojzë e Atlantikut Verior (f)	[ʃójzə ɛ atlantíkut vɛrjór]
ham	sallam (m)	[saɫám]
hamburger	hamburger (m)	[hamburgér]
hamburger	hamburger	[hamburgér]
hazelnut	lajthi (f)	[lajθí]
herring	harengë (f)	[haréŋə]
honey	mjaltë (f)	[mjáɫtə]
horseradish	rrepë djegëse (f)	[répə djégəsɛ]
hot	i nxehtë	[i ndzéhtə]
ice	akull (m)	[ákuɫ]
ice-cream	akullore (f)	[akuɫórɛ]
instant coffee	neskafe (f)	[nɛskáfɛ]
jam	reçel (m)	[rɛtʃél]
jam	reçel (m)	[rɛtʃél]
juice	lëng frutash (m)	[ləŋ frútaʃ]
kidney bean	groshë (f)	[gróʃə]
kiwi	kivi (m)	[kívi]
knife	thikë (f)	[θíkə]
lamb	mish qengji (m)	[miʃ cénɟi]
lemon	limon (m)	[limón]
lemonade	limonadë (f)	[limonádə]
lentil	thjerrëz (f)	[θjérəz]
lettuce	sallatë jeshile (f)	[saɫátə jɛʃílɛ]
light beer	birrë e lehtë (f)	[bírə ɛ léhtə]
liqueur	liker (m)	[likér]
liquors	likere (pl)	[likérɛ]
liver	mëlçi (f)	[məltʃí]
lunch	drekë (f)	[drékə]
mackerel	skumbri (m)	[skúmbri]
mandarin	mandarinë (f)	[mandarínə]
mango	mango (f)	[máŋo]
margarine	margarinë (f)	[margarínə]
marmalade	marmelatë (f)	[marmɛlátə]
mashed potatoes	pure patatesh (f)	[puré patátɛʃ]
mayonnaise	majonezë (f)	[majonézə]
meat	mish (m)	[miʃ]
melon	pjepër (m)	[pjépər]
menu	menu (f)	[mɛnú]
milk	qumësht (m)	[cúməʃt]
milkshake	milkshake (f)	[milkʃákɛ]
millet	mel (m)	[mɛl]
mineral water	ujë mineral (m)	[újə minɛrál]
morel	morele (f)	[morélɛ]
mushroom	kërpudhë (f)	[kərpúðə]
mustard	mustardë (f)	[mustárdə]
non-alcoholic	jo alkoolik	[jo alkoolík]
noodles	makarona petë (f)	[makaróna pétə]
oats	tërshërë (f)	[tərʃérə]
olive oil	vaj ulliri (m)	[vaj uɫíri]
olives	ullinj (pl)	[uɫíɲ]
omelet	omëletë (f)	[oməlétə]

onion	qepë (f)	[cépə]
orange	portokall (m)	[portokáł]
orange juice	lëng portokalli (m)	[ləŋ portokáłi]
orange-cap boletus	kërpudhë kapuç-verdhë (f)	[kərpúðə kapútʃ-vérðə]
oyster	midhje (f)	[míðjɛ]
pâté	pate (f)	[paté]
papaya	papaja (f)	[papája]
paprika	spec (m)	[spɛts]
parsley	majdanoz (m)	[majdanóz]
pasta	makarona (f)	[makaróna]
pea	bizele (f)	[bizélɛ]
peach	pjeshkë (f)	[pjéʃkə]
peanut	kikirik (m)	[kikirík]
pear	dardhë (f)	[dárðə]
peel	lëkurë (f)	[ləkúrə]
perch	perç (m)	[pɛrtʃ]
pickled	i marinuar	[i marinúar]
pie	tortë (f)	[tórtə]
piece	copë (f)	[tsópə]
pike	mlysh (m)	[mlýʃ]
pike perch	troftë (f)	[tróftə]
pineapple	ananas (m)	[ananás]
pistachios	fëstëk (m)	[fəsták]
pizza	pica (f)	[pítsa]
plate	pjatë (f)	[pjátə]
plum	kumbull (f)	[kúmbuł]
poisonous mushroom	kërpudhë helmuese (f)	[kərpúðə hɛlmúɛsɛ]
pomegranate	shegë (f)	[ʃégə]
pork	mish derri (m)	[miʃ déri]
porridge	qull (m)	[cuł]
portion	racion (m)	[ratsión]
potato	patate (f)	[patátɛ]
proteins	proteinë (f)	[protɛínə]
pub, bar	pab (m), pijetore (f)	[pab], [pijɛtórɛ]
pudding	puding (m)	[pudíŋ]
pumpkin	kungull (m)	[kúŋuł]
rabbit	mish lepuri (m)	[miʃ lépuri]
radish	rrepkë (f)	[répkə]
raisin	rrush i thatë (m)	[ruʃ i θátə]
raspberry	mjedër (f)	[mjédər]
recipe	recetë (f)	[rɛtsétə]
red pepper	piper i kuq (m)	[pipér i kuc]
red wine	verë e kuqe (f)	[vérə ɛ kúcɛ]
redcurrant	kaliboba e kuqe (f)	[kalibóba ɛ kúcɛ]
refreshing drink	pije freskuese (f)	[píjɛ frɛskúɛsɛ]
rice	oriz (m)	[oríz]
rum	rum (m)	[rum]
russula	rusula (f)	[rúsula]
rye	thekër (f)	[θékər]
saffron	shafran (m)	[ʃafrán]
salad	sallatë (f)	[sałátə]

salmon	salmon (m)	[salmón]
salt	kripë (f)	[krípə]
salty	i kripur	[i krípur]
sandwich	sandviç (m)	[sandvítʃ]
sardine	sardele (f)	[sardélɛ]
sauce	salcë (f)	[sáltsə]
saucer	pjatë filxhani (f)	[pjátə fildʒáni]
sausage	salsiçe (f)	[salsítʃɛ]
seafood	fruta deti (pl)	[frúta déti]
sesame	susam (m)	[susám]
shark	peshkaqen (m)	[pɛʃkacén]
shrimp	karkalec (m)	[karkaléts]
side dish	garniturë (f)	[garnitúrə]
slice	fetë (f)	[fétə]
smoked	i tymosur	[i tymósur]
soft drink	pije e lehtë (f)	[píjɛ ɛ léhtə]
soup	supë (f)	[súpə]
soup spoon	lugë gjelle (f)	[lúgə ɟéłɛ]
sour cherry	qershi vishnje (f)	[cɛrʃí víʃɲɛ]
sour cream	salcë kosi (f)	[sáltsə kosi]
soy	sojë (f)	[sójə]
spaghetti	shpageti (pl)	[ʃpagéti]
sparkling	ujë i gazuar	[újə i gazúar]
spice	erëz (f)	[érəz]
spinach	spinaq (m)	[spinác]
spiny lobster	karavidhe (f)	[karavíðɛ]
spoon	lugë (f)	[lúgə]
squid	kallamarë (f)	[kałamárə]
steak	biftek (m)	[bifték]
still	ujë natyral	[újə natyrál]
strawberry	luleshtrydhe (f)	[lułɛʃtrýðɛ]
sturgeon	bli (m)	[bli]
sugar	sheqer (m)	[ʃecér]
sunflower oil	vaj luledielli (m)	[vaj lułɛdiéłi]
sweet	i ëmbël	[i émbəl]
sweet cherry	qershi (f)	[cɛrʃí]
taste, flavor	shije (f)	[ʃíjɛ]
tasty	i shijshëm	[i ʃíjʃəm]
tea	çaj (m)	[tʃáj]
teaspoon	lugë çaji (f)	[lúgə tʃáji]
tip	bakshish (m)	[bakʃíʃ]
tomato	domate (f)	[domátɛ]
tomato juice	lëng domatesh (m)	[ləŋ domátɛʃ]
tongue	gjuhë (f)	[ɟúhə]
toothpick	kruajtëse dhëmbësh (f)	[krúajtəsɛ ðémbəʃ]
trout	troftë (f)	[tróftə]
tuna	tunë (f)	[túnə]
turkey	mish gjel deti (m)	[miʃ ɟɛl déti]
turnip	rrepë (f)	[répə]
veal	mish viçi (m)	[miʃ vítʃi]
vegetable oil	vaj vegjetal (m)	[vaj vɛɟɛtál]
vegetables	perime (pl)	[pɛrímɛ]

vegetarian	**vegjetarian** (m)	[vɛɟɛtarián]
vegetarian	**vegjetarian**	[vɛɟɛtarián]
vermouth	**vermut** (m)	[vɛrmút]
vienna sausage	**salsiçe vjeneze** (f)	[salsítʃɛ vjɛnézɛ]
vinegar	**uthull** (f)	[úθuɫ]
vitamin	**vitaminë** (f)	[vitamínə]
vodka	**vodkë** (f)	[vódkə]
wafers	**vafera** (pl)	[vaféra]
waiter	**kamerier** (m)	[kamɛriér]
waitress	**kameriere** (f)	[kamɛriérɛ]
walnut	**arrë** (f)	[árə]
water	**ujë** (m)	[újə]
watermelon	**shalqi** (m)	[ʃalcí]
wheat	**grurë** (f)	[grúrə]
whiskey	**uiski** (m)	[víski]
white wine	**verë e bardhë** (f)	[vérə ɛ bárðə]
wild strawberry	**luleshtrydhe e egër** (f)	[lulɛʃtrýðɛ ɛ égər]
wine	**verë** (f)	[vérə]
wine list	**menu vererash** (f)	[mɛnú vérəraʃ]
with ice	**me akull**	[mɛ ákuɫ]
yogurt	**kos** (m)	[kos]
zucchini	**kungulleshë** (m)	[kuŋuɫéʃə]

Albanian-English gastronomic glossary

çaj (m)	[tʃáj]	tea
çaj i zi (m)	[tʃáj i zí]	black tea
çaj jeshil (m)	[tʃáj jɛʃíl]	green tea
çamçakëz (m)	[tʃamtʃakéz]	chewing gum
çokollatë (f)	[tʃokołátə]	chocolate
ëmbëlsirë (f)	[əmbəlsírə]	dessert
ëmbëlsira (pl)	[əmbəlsíra]	confectionery
akull (m)	[ákuł]	ice
akullore (f)	[akułórɛ]	ice-cream
ananas (m)	[ananás]	pineapple
angjinare (f)	[anɟinárɛ]	artichoke
anisetë (f)	[anisétə]	anise
antipastë (f)	[antipástə]	appetizer
aperitiv (m)	[apɛritív]	aperitif
arrë (f)	[árə]	walnut
arrë kokosi (f)	[árə kokósi]	coconut
asparagus (m)	[asparágus]	asparagus
avokado (f)	[avokádo]	avocado
bajame (f)	[bajámɛ]	almond
bakshish (m)	[bakʃíʃ]	tip
banakier (m)	[banakiéɾ]	bartender
banane (f)	[banánɛ]	banana
biftek (m)	[bifték]	steak
birrë (f)	[bírə]	beer
birrë e lehtë (f)	[bírə ɛ léhtə]	light beer
birrë e zezë (f)	[bírə ɛ zézə]	dark beer
biskota (pl)	[biskóta]	cookies
bizele (f)	[bizélɛ]	pea
bli (m)	[blí]	sturgeon
boronicë (f)	[boronítsə]	bilberry
boronicë mirtile (f)	[boronítsə mirtílɛ]	cowberry
boronica (f)	[boronítsa]	cranberry
borzilok (m)	[borzilók]	basil
brokoli (m)	[brókoli]	broccoli
bukë (f)	[búkə]	bread
copë (f)	[tsópə]	piece
dardhë (f)	[dárðə]	pear
darkë (f)	[dárkə]	dinner
dietë (f)	[diétə]	diet
djath (m)	[djáθ]	cheese
domate (f)	[domátɛ]	tomato
drekë (f)	[drékə]	lunch
drithë (m)	[dríθə]	grain
drithëra (pl)	[dríθəra]	groats

drithëra (pl)	[dríθǝra]	cereal crops
dromcë (f)	[drómtsǝ]	crumb
e bardhë veze (f)	[ɛ bárðǝ vézɛ]	egg white
e verdhë veze (f)	[ɛ vérðǝ vézɛ]	egg yolk
elb (m)	[ɛlb]	barley
erëz (f)	[érǝz]	spice
fëstëk (m)	[fǝsték]	pistachios
fasule (f)	[fasúlɛ]	beans
faturë (f)	[fatúrǝ]	check
fetë (f)	[fétǝ]	slice
fik (m)	[fik]	fig
filxhan (m)	[fildʒán]	cup
frut (m)	[frut]	fruit
fruta (pl)	[frúta]	fruits
fruta deti (pl)	[frúta déti]	seafood
gaforre (f)	[gafórɛ]	crab
garniturë (f)	[garnitúrǝ]	side dish
gjah (m)	[ɟáh]	game
gjalp (m)	[ɟalp]	butter
gjeth dafine (m)	[ɟɛθ dafínɛ]	bay leaf
gjuhë (f)	[ɟúhǝ]	tongue
gotë (f)	[gótǝ]	glass
gotë vere (f)	[gótǝ vérɛ]	glass
grejpfrut (m)	[grɛjpfrút]	grapefruit
groshë (f)	[gróʃǝ]	kidney bean
grurë (f)	[grúrǝ]	wheat
hamburger	[hamburgér]	hamburger
hamburger (m)	[hamburgér]	hamburger
hapëse kanoçesh (f)	[hapǝsé kanótʃɛʃ]	can opener
hapëse shishesh (f)	[hapǝsé ʃíʃɛʃ]	bottle opener
harengë (f)	[harénǝ]	herring
havjar (m)	[havjár]	caviar
hikërr (m)	[híkǝr]	buckwheat
hudhër (f)	[húðǝr]	garlic
hurmë (f)	[húrmǝ]	date
i ëmbël	[i émbǝl]	sweet
i ftohtë	[i ftóhtǝ]	cold
i hidhur	[i híður]	bitter
i kripur	[i krípur]	salty
i marinuar	[i marinúar]	pickled
i ngrirë	[i ŋrírǝ]	frozen
i nxehtë	[i ndzéhtǝ]	hot
i shijshëm	[i ʃíjʃǝm]	tasty
i skuqur	[i skúcur]	fried
i tharë	[i θárǝ]	dried
i tymosur	[i tymósur]	smoked
i zier	[i zíɛr]	boiled
jo alkoolik	[jo alkoolík]	non-alcoholic
kërpudhë (f)	[kǝrpúðǝ]	mushroom
kërpudhë helmuese (f)	[kǝrpúðǝ hɛlmúɛsɛ]	poisonous mushroom
kërpudhë kapuç-verdhë (f)	[kǝrpúðǝ kapútʃ-vérðǝ]	orange-cap boletus

kërpudhë ushqyese (f)	[kərpúðə uʃcýɛsɛ]	edible mushroom
kërpudha e vdekjes (f)	[kərpúða ɛ vdékjɛs]	death cap
kësulkuqe (f)	[kəsulkúcɛ]	fly agaric
kafe (f)	[káfɛ]	coffee
kafe e zezë (f)	[káfɛ ɛ zézə]	black coffee
kafe me qumësht (m)	[káfɛ mɛ cúməʃt]	coffee with milk
kajsi (f)	[kajsí]	apricot
kaliboba e kuqe (f)	[kalibóba ɛ kúcɛ]	redcurrant
kaliboba e zezë (f)	[kalibóba ɛ zézə]	blackcurrant
kallamarë (f)	[kałamárə]	squid
kalori (f)	[kalorí]	calorie
kamerier (m)	[kamɛriéɾ]	waiter
kameriere (f)	[kamɛriérɛ]	waitress
kanellë (f)	[kanéłə]	cinnamon
kapuçino (m)	[kaputʃíno]	cappuccino
karafil (m)	[karafíl]	cloves
karamele (f)	[karamélɛ]	candy
karavidhe (f)	[karavíðɛ]	spiny lobster
karbohidrat (m)	[karbohidrát]	carbohydrates
karkalec (m)	[karkaléts]	shrimp
karotë (f)	[karótə]	carrot
kastravec (m)	[kastravéts]	cucumber
kaush (m)	[kaúʃ]	ear
kek (m)	[kék]	cake
kikirik (m)	[kikiрík]	peanut
kivi (m)	[kívi]	kiwi
kofshë derri (f)	[kófʃə déri]	gammon
koktej (m)	[koktéj]	cocktail
konjak (m)	[koɲák]	cognac
konserva (f)	[konsérva]	canned food
kopër (f)	[kópər]	dill
koriandër (m)	[koriándəɾ]	coriander
kornfleiks (m)	[kornfléiks]	cornflakes
kos (m)	[kos]	yogurt
krap (m)	[krap]	carp
krapuliq (m)	[krapulíc]	bream
krem gjalpi (m)	[krɛm ɟálpi]	buttercream
krem qumështi (m)	[krɛm cúməʃti]	cream
kripë (f)	[krípə]	salt
kruajtëse dhëmbësh (f)	[krúajtəsɛ ðémbəʃ]	toothpick
krustace (pl)	[krustátsɛ]	crustaceans
kulumbri (f)	[kulumbrí]	gooseberry
kumbull (f)	[kúmbuł]	plum
kumin (m)	[kumín]	caraway
kungull (m)	[kúɲuł]	pumpkin
kungulleshë (m)	[kuɲułéʃə]	zucchini
kuzhinë (f)	[kuʒínə]	cuisine
lëkurë (f)	[ləkúrə]	peel
lëng domatesh (m)	[ləŋ domátɛʃ]	tomato juice
lëng frutash (m)	[ləŋ frútaʃ]	juice
lëng frutash i freskët (m)	[ləŋ frútaʃ i fréskət]	freshly squeezed juice
lëng mishi (m)	[ləŋ míʃi]	clear soup

lëng portokalli (m)	[ləŋ portokáti]	orange juice
lajthi (f)	[lajθí]	hazelnut
lakër (f)	[lákər]	cabbage
lakër Brukseli (f)	[lákər brukséli]	Brussels sprouts
liker (m)	[likér]	liqueur
likere (pl)	[likérɛ]	liquors
limon (m)	[limón]	lemon
limonadë (f)	[limonádə]	lemonade
lugë çaji (f)	[lúgə tʃáji]	teaspoon
lugë (f)	[lúgə]	spoon
lugë gjelle (f)	[lúgə ɟétɛ]	soup spoon
lulelakër (f)	[lulɛlákər]	cauliflower
luleshtrydhe (f)	[lulɛʃtrýðɛ]	strawberry
luleshtrydhe e egër (f)	[lulɛʃtrýðɛ ɛ égər]	wild strawberry
mëlçi (f)	[məltʃí]	liver
mëngjes (m)	[mənɟés]	breakfast
majdanoz (m)	[majdanóz]	parsley
majonezë (f)	[majonézə]	mayonnaise
makarona (f)	[makaróna]	pasta
makarona petë (f)	[makaróna pétə]	noodles
manë (f)	[mánə]	berry
mana (f)	[mána]	berries
manaferra (f)	[manaférra]	blackberry
mandarinë (f)	[mandarínə]	mandarin
mango (f)	[máŋo]	mango
margarinë (f)	[margarínə]	margarine
marmelatë (f)	[marmɛlátə]	marmalade
mbushje (f)	[mbúʃjɛ]	filling
me akull	[mɛ ákut]	with ice
mel (m)	[mɛl]	millet
menu (f)	[mɛnú]	menu
menu verërash (f)	[mɛnú vérəraʃ]	wine list
merluc (m)	[mɛrlúts]	cod
midhje (f)	[míðjɛ]	oyster
miell (m)	[míɛt]	flour
milkshake (f)	[milkʃákɛ]	milkshake
misër (m)	[mísər]	corn
misër (m)	[mísər]	corn
mish (m)	[miʃ]	meat
mish derri (m)	[miʃ déri]	pork
mish gjel deti (m)	[miʃ ɟɛl déti]	turkey
mish lepuri (m)	[miʃ lépuri]	rabbit
mish lope (m)	[miʃ lópɛ]	beef
mish qengji (m)	[miʃ cénɟi]	lamb
mish viçi (m)	[miʃ vítʃi]	veal
mjaltë (f)	[mjáltə]	honey
mjedër (f)	[mjédər]	raspberry
mlysh (m)	[mlýʃ]	pike
mollë (f)	[mótə]	apple
morele (f)	[morélɛ]	morel
mustak (m)	[musták]	catfish
mustardë (f)	[mustárdə]	mustard

neskafe (f)	[nɛskáfɛ]	instant coffee
ngjalë (f)	[nɟálə]	eel
omëletë (f)	[oməlétə]	omelet
oreks (m)	[oréks]	appetite
oriz (m)	[oríz]	rice
pab (m), pijetore (f)	[pab], [pijɛtórɛ]	pub, bar
panxhar (m)	[pandʒár]	beet
papaja (f)	[papája]	papaya
patë (f)	[pátə]	goose
patëllxhan (m)	[patətdʒán]	eggplant
patate (f)	[patátɛ]	potato
pate (f)	[paté]	pâté
perç (m)	[pɛrtʃ]	perch
perime (pl)	[pɛrímɛ]	vegetables
peshk (m)	[pɛʃk]	fish
peshkaqen (m)	[pɛʃkacén]	shark
pica (f)	[pítsa]	pizza
pije e lehtë (f)	[píjɛ ɛ léhtə]	soft drink
pije freskuese (f)	[píjɛ frɛskúɛsɛ]	refreshing drink
piper i kuq (m)	[pipér i kuc]	red pepper
piper i zi (m)	[pipér i zi]	black pepper
pirun (m)	[pirún]	fork
pjatë (f)	[pjátə]	course, dish
pjatë (f)	[pjátə]	plate
pjatë filxhani (f)	[pjátə fildʒáni]	saucer
pjepër (m)	[pjépər]	melon
pjeshkë (f)	[pjéʃkə]	peach
porcinela (f)	[portsinéla]	birch bolete
porcini (m)	[portsíni]	cep
portokall (m)	[portokátɬ]	orange
prej çokollate	[prɛj tʃokotátɛ]	chocolate
proshutë (f)	[proʃútə]	bacon
proteinë (f)	[protɛínə]	proteins
puding (m)	[pudíŋ]	pudding
pulë (f)	[púlə]	chicken
pure patatesh (f)	[puré patátɛʃ]	mashed potatoes
qepë (f)	[cépə]	onion
qershi (f)	[cɛrʃí]	sweet cherry
qershi vishnje (f)	[cɛrʃí víʃɲɛ]	sour cherry
qull (m)	[cutɬ]	porridge
qumësht (m)	[cúməʃt]	milk
qumësht i kondensuar (m)	[cúməʃt i kondɛnsúar]	condensed milk
racion (m)	[ratsión]	portion
reçel (m)	[rɛtʃél]	jam
reçel (m)	[rɛtʃél]	jam
recetë (f)	[rɛtsétə]	recipe
rosë (f)	[rósə]	duck
rrepë (f)	[répə]	turnip
rrepë djegëse (f)	[répə djégəsɛ]	horseradish
rrepkë (f)	[répkə]	radish
rrush (m)	[ruʃ]	grape
rrush i thatë (m)	[ruʃ i θátə]	raisin

rum (m)	[rum]	rum
rusula (f)	[rúsula]	russula
salcë (f)	[sáltsə]	condiment
salcë (f)	[sáltsə]	sauce
salcë kosi (f)	[sáltsə kosi]	sour cream
sallam (m)	[saɫám]	ham
sallatë (f)	[saɫátə]	salad
sallatë jeshile (f)	[saɫátə jɛʃílɛ]	lettuce
salmon (m)	[salmón]	salmon
salmon Atlantiku (m)	[salmón atlantíku]	Atlantic salmon
salsiçe (f)	[salsítʃɛ]	sausage
salsiçe vjeneze (f)	[salsítʃɛ vjɛnézɛ]	vienna sausage
sandviç (m)	[sandvítʃ]	sandwich
sardele (f)	[sardélɛ]	sardine
selino (f)	[sɛlíno]	celery
shafran (m)	[ʃafrán]	saffron
shalqi (m)	[ʃalcí]	watermelon
shampanjë (f)	[ʃampáɲə]	champagne
shanterele (f)	[ʃantɛrélɛ]	chanterelle
shegë (f)	[ʃégə]	pomegranate
sheqer (m)	[ʃɛcér]	sugar
shije (f)	[ʃíjɛ]	taste, flavor
shije (f)	[ʃíjɛ]	aftertaste
shojzë (f)	[ʃójzə]	flatfish
shojzë e Atlantikut Verior (f)	[ʃójzə ɛ atlantíkut vɛriór]	halibut
shpageti (pl)	[ʃpagéti]	spaghetti
skumbri (m)	[skúmbri]	mackerel
sojë (f)	[sójə]	soy
spec (m)	[spɛts]	bell pepper
spec (m)	[spɛts]	paprika
spinaq (m)	[spinác]	spinach
supë (f)	[súpə]	soup
susam (m)	[susám]	sesame
Të bëftë mirë!	[tə bəftə mírə!]	Enjoy your meal!
tërshërë (f)	[tərʃérə]	oats
thekër (m)	[θékər]	rye
thikë (f)	[θíkə]	knife
thjerrëz (f)	[θjérəz]	lentil
tortë (f)	[tórtə]	cake
tortë (f)	[tórtə]	pie
troftë (f)	[tróftə]	trout
troftë (f)	[tróftə]	pike perch
tunë (f)	[túnə]	tuna
turjelë tapash (f)	[turjélə tápaʃ]	corkscrew
uiski (m)	[víski]	whiskey
ujë (m)	[újə]	water
ujë i gazuar	[újə i gazúar]	sparkling
ujë i karbonuar	[újə i karbonúar]	carbonated
ujë i pijshëm (m)	[újə i píjʃəm]	drinking water
ujë mineral (m)	[újə minɛrál]	mineral water
ujë natyral	[újə natyrál]	still

ullinj (pl)	[utíɲ]	olives
ushqim (m)	[uʃcím]	food
uthull (f)	[úθuɬ]	vinegar
vafera (pl)	[vaféra]	wafers
vaj luledielli (m)	[vaj lulɛdiéti]	sunflower oil
vaj ulliri (m)	[vaj utíri]	olive oil
vaj vegjetal (m)	[vaj vɛɟɛtál]	vegetable oil
ve (f)	[vɛ]	egg
vegjetarian	[vɛɟɛtarián]	vegetarian
vegjetarian (m)	[vɛɟɛtarián]	vegetarian
verë (f)	[vérə]	wine
verë e bardhë (f)	[vérə ɛ bárðə]	white wine
verë e kuqe (f)	[vérə ɛ kúcɛ]	red wine
vermut (m)	[vɛrmút]	vermouth
vezë (pl)	[vézə]	eggs
vezë të skuqura (pl)	[vézə tə skúcura]	fried eggs
vitaminë (f)	[vitamínə]	vitamin
vodkë (f)	[vódkə]	vodka
xhenxhefil (m)	[dʒɛndʒɛfíl]	ginger
xhin (m)	[dʒin]	gin
yndyrë (f)	[yndýrə]	fats
zarzavate (pl)	[zarzavátɛ]	greens